Chinese Love Signs

Neil Somerville

D0954316

Thorsons

An Imprint of HarperCollins*Publishers*

Thorsons
An Imprint of HarperCollins*Publishers*
77–85 Fulham Palace Road,
Hammersmith, London W6 8JB
1160 Battery Street,
San Francisco, California 94111–1213

Published by Thorsons 1995
1   3   5   7   9   10   8   6   4   2

Neil Somerville asserts the moral right to
be identified as the author of this work

A catalogue record for this book
is available from the British Library

ISBN 1 85538 405 1

Printed by HarperCollinsManufacturing Glasgow

CONTENTS

Contents

I was born under the sign of the Snake, my wife under the sign of the Monkey and my two children under the signs of the Ox and Horse. With such a splendid mix of Chinese signs, life is never dull!

To Ros, Richard and Emily, thank you for all your support and love.

Neil Somerville has been interested in Chinese horoscopes and Eastern methods of divination for many years. He is the author of the best-selling annual publication *Your Chinese Horoscope*. He has also compiled several puzzle books and has written for magazines and newspapers.

INTRODUCTION

C hinese astrology has been practised for thousands of years and plays an important part in the lives of millions of people in the Far East. However, it is only recently that we in the West have been able to discover and appreciate the wonders and fascination of this ancient art.

In Chinese astrology there are 12 different signs. Each sign is named after an animal and each animal sign rules a year. Those born in that year inherit some of the characteristics of the animal. For instance, people born in the Monkey year tend to be enterprising and resourceful, like the Monkey, and people born in the year of the Ox are tenacious and hard-working, just like the Ox. There are, of course, other factors which can affect the personality of the sign – these include the element ruling the year of birth and the ascendant, or time of birth. This helps to explain why some born under the same sign can appear so different to others. However, rather than complicate the text with the effects of the elements and ascendants, I have concentrated on the broad personality traits for each of the signs and I believe these will give you a good understanding of the nature of your own sign.

To find out your sign, check the year you were born in the table of Chinese years (*see pages 231–3*). The Chinese calendar is based on the lunar year and starts late in January or early February.

Part I of the book contains a description of the main characteristics of the 12 signs and Part II examines the relationship between the signs. You will be able to check on your own personality traits and discover which sign is most compatible to your own and which could bring you the most happiness in friendship, love and marriage. The ways in which the signs relate to each other in working situations and as parent and child are also described.

It is fascinating to find out how the signs react to each other and I hope that this book will go some way to indicating why you get on well with some people but can have personality clashes with others. Even if you find that those close to you have signs not regarded as fully compatible with your own, at least you may be alerted to possible problem areas and may be able to avert future differences. I hop\ *Chinese Love Signs* will prove both illuminating and helpful.

Much has been written in recent years about the Chinese signs but to this day no one knows exactly how they originated. One legend speaks of Buddha inviting the animals of the kingdom to a New Year Party. Only 12 animals decided to go and in grati-tude Buddha named a year after each animal. Another legend offers an explanation for the order of years. In this, the animals had to race across a river and the order they finished would be the order of years. The Rat, ever an opportunist and determined to win, craftily rode on the back of the Ox and just as the Ox reached the river bank, the Rat leapt off in front of him and won the race. This, according to the story, is why the Rat starts the cycle of years; the Ox is next and then come the other 10 animals. The Pig, always one to enjoy himself, came in last!

Some books on Chinese astrology refer to some of the signs by different names although the personality of the sign remains the same. The Ox has been referred to as the Buffalo or Bull, the Rabbit as the Hare or Cat, the Goat as the Sheep or Ram, the Rooster as the Cock and the Pig as the Boar.

I have also had to address the thorny problem of how to refer to the signs – whether to use masculine gender, to refer to the signs as 'he or she' or the more neutral 'they'. I have opted for the 'he', but unless otherwise stated this term covers both the male and female of the sign.

I believe that the 12 Chinese signs can teach us much about ourselves and our relations with those around us and hope that you will find *Chinese Love Signs* instructive, informative and enjoyable reading.

Those who love others are always loved in return.

CHINESE PROVERB

Part One

THE CHINESE SIGNS

THE RAT

Key characteristics: Charming, sociable, resourceful, quick-witted, ambitious, opportunistic, versatile, perceptive, thrifty and crafty.

In love: Romantic, attentive, affectionate – and hard to resist!

Although the rat may not be generally considered the most endearing of creatures, the rat is immensely resourceful, intelligent and alert. The rat is quick to spot and take advantage of any opportunity that it sees and is resilient and strong willed. Many of these traits are found in those born under the first of the Chinese signs.

The Rat is governed by charm. He has a friendly and sociable manner and a good understanding of human nature. The Rat knows how to put others at ease and is invariably popular and has many friends.

The Rat has wide interests, is a keen socializer and enjoys attending parties and functions. He has a good appreciation of the finer things in life and can be a connoisseur of good food and drink. He is also an eloquent and persuasive speaker and with his alert and penetrating mind, his opinions are often sought. The Rat is most perceptive and if you are asking for a frank and honest opinion his views are hard to beat. The Rat makes a good critic.

However, although the Rat appears confident and self-assured there is another side to his character. For all his charm and bonhomie he can be crafty, manipulative and driven by ambition. He likes to keep himself continually busy and one of his main aims in life is to improve upon his present situation. The Rat is a supreme opportunist and if he sees a situation which he feels he can turn to his advantage he is sure to act. He is quick-witted, certainly resourceful and not averse to taking the occasional risk.

The Rat is also a hard and industrious worker although he is generally more suited to intellectual rather than manual work. He particularly excels in positions which bring him into contact with others and he can do well in marketing, selling, PR work and accountancy. As they are observant and good at communicating their views, Rats can make fine writers and also do well in any position where they have a certain freedom to act and can follow their own initiative. If, however, the Rat finds himself in a too restrictive or bureaucratic environment he can very easily become pernickety, regimented and a stickler for the rule book.

In addition to being conscientious in his work, the Rat is careful when dealing with money matters. He is often thrifty and keeps a close watch over his finances. However, despite his careful manner, the Rat can be most indulgent and finds it hard to resist buying anything that he might want. After scrimping and saving his money for some time he could quite easily be tempted to spend out on a sudden whim. Generally, however, the Rat is prudent in money matters and while to some he might appear tight-fisted, he can be most generous to his family members and those close to him.

Although the Rat is able to gain the confidence of others well, he is however a private individual. He will not allow others to pry too closely into his own concerns and he likes to retain a certain independence in his actions. The Rat likes to be responsible to no one but himself and he relies a great deal on his wits. Should he ever find himself in a difficult situation he is usually most adept at extracting himself from it. The Rat is a survivor and even when events go against him, he will often be the first to pick up the pieces and look for new challenges and opportunities. He just loves keeping himself busy and fully occupied –

no matter whether it is to do with work, his social life or his family.

Being so sociable, the Rat values his relations with others and he makes friends with ease. He has a particularly romantic nature and is passionate, tender and caring. In love, he will do all he can to win and retain the source of his affection – and he usually succeeds. The Rat is mos supportive to his partner and will invariably try to establish a close-knit family. Family bonds are important to the Rat and even though he may have left home early, he will always maintain close links with his parents. The Rat is a good homemaker and his abode will be comfortable and tastefully furnished. The Rat does, however, have a tendency to hoard – he hates waste and dislikes throwing anything away lest it comes in useful later. As a consequence, although his home may appear reasonably orderly, his cupboards are often full to overflowing.

When possible, the Rat tends to have a large family and he makes a loving and caring parent. With his wide interests and fertile imagination he will encourage his children but will also be a good disciplinarian. The Rat relates well to children and his children can gain much from having an attentive and enterprising Rat as a parent.

The female Rat has a lively and outgoing manner. She has an alert mind and, with her winning personality, can do well in her chosen profession. However, no matter how successful she might be, her family is always her first priority. In appearance she is smart and chooses stylish and fashionable clothes. The female Rat certainly knows how to make the most of her often striking looks.

The male Rate is outgoing, suave and confident. However, behind his gracious and personable manner there lurks a sharp mind and a strong ambitious nature. The male Rat can be disarmingly persuasive and is adept at getting what he wants.

Despite the Rat's many fine qualities, he also has his weaknesses. In his desire to do well he can be greedy and sometimes find himself involved in more activities than he can properly handle. At times he can be petty, but the Rat controls his feelings well and often the less appealing aspects of his nature remain well hidden.

In view of his range of talents, the Rat's life can take many courses. However, his childhood and youth will generally be a happy and enjoyable time. As a child he has an alert and curious mind. He will delight in learning new feats and has an outgoing and adventurous nature. He often does well at school and assimilates information quickly. He is popular and one of the 'in crowd'. However, while the Rat child may seem confident and self-assured, he is still in need of much love and support. He values and loves his parents dearly and strives to please them; in return he greatly needs their affection. Without it his confidence, zest and lively spirit may be greatly undermined.

In his youth the Rat will not only delight in the challenges and opportunities that are before him but will also savour the delights of love. He has a strong sexual drive and affairs of the heart are most important to him.

When he settles down the Rat will aim to establish a secure and stable home life. He will become more preoccupied with material concerns and endeavour to improve and better his position. Sometimes his ventures meet with success but there will be occasions when he lets his opportunism get the better of him and he makes unwise decisions. In adulthood the Rat can experience success and also failure. However, he is resilient and quickly learns from experience. The Rat rarely makes the same mistake twice.

In old age the Rat will be able to reap the rewards of his efforts. He will have his family, his many friends, numerous interests and be able to enjoy a comfortable lifestyle.

The Rat has the distinction of being the first sign in the Chinese zodiac and, with his charm and personable manner, he is invariably popular and well respected. The British Prime Minister Benjamin Disraeli was a Rat and a supreme opportunist. He once declared, 'Life is too short to be little', and this maxim holds good for many Rats. The Rat is one who certainly makes the most of his life.

Famous Rats

Alan Alda, Dave Allen, Ursula Andress, Charles Aznavour, Lauren Bacall, Shirley Bassey, Jeremy Beadle, Kenneth Branagh, Marlon Brando, Charlotte Bronte, Chris de Burgh, George Bush, Jimmy Carter, Dick Cavett, Maurice Chevalier, Barbara Dickson, Noel Edmonds, Ben Elton, Albert Finney, Clark Gable, Al Gore, Thomas Hardy, Mata Hari, Vaclav Havel, Charlton Heston, Dennis Hopper, Englebert Humperdinck, Jeremy Irons, Glenda Jackson, Jean-Michel Jarre, Gene Kelly, Kris Kristofferson, Sir Andrew Lloyd Webber, Lulu, Richard Nixon, Sean Penn, The Queen Mother, Vanessa Redgrave, Burt Reynolds, Jonathan Ross, Emma Samms, William Shakespeare, Tommy Steele, Donna Summer, Spencer Tracey, the Prince of Wales, George Washington, Dennis Waterman, Kim Wilde, the Duke of York.

THE OX

Key characteristics: Resolute, strong willed, determined, ambitious, tenacious, methodical, careful, patient, persevering, but stubborn and intransigent.

In love: Loyal, caring and dependable.

W hether ploughing a field or pulling a cart, the ox is a strong and disciplined worker. He sets about his tasks in a responsible and dutiful manner and these qualities are often found in people born under the second of the Chinese signs.

The Ox is governed by equilibrium and tenacity. He has a calm, quiet and orderly manner and while he may appear reserved, he is both resolute and tenacious. The Ox may not be overly demonstrative in his emotions, but he is very sure of himself and knows what he wants in life.

The Ox sets about life in a cautious and methodical way. He plans his activities carefully and does not like change or anything too gimmicky or innovative. The Ox is a traditionalist and conservative in outlook. He has an honest and trusting nature and is open in his views. He is a down-to-earth sort of person and while he may sometimes lack tact, at least those who come in contact with him know exactly where he stands. He will never commit himself to undertakings which he knows he cannot fulfil and is realistic in his ambitions and expectations.

The Ox also has a most patient and persevering nature and will strive long and hard until he has achieved his objectives. The Ox is methodical, diligent and often a loner. He likes to conduct his activities in his own way and to his own exacting

standards. The Ox also prefers to specialize and have set interests rather than engage in a wide variety of activities. In some
ways, the Ox is unadventurous, but his life will be stable and
well ordered. In all his activities, in his home, his personal life
and his work, the Ox is responsible and careful.

The Ox often does well in his chosen career. He is conscientious and is much admired for his calm, confident and resolute
nature. Often he will have decided at an early age what he wants
to do and will specialize in a certain line of work. With his
resolute and principled manner, the Ox often rises to the top of
his profession and can enjoy success in politics, medicine, the
law or, with his practical nature, as a skilled technician or engin-
eer. Many Oxen have a fine ear for music and some have excelled
in musical careers. The Ox also has a strong affinity with the land
and can do particularly well in farming or estate management.
He may not, however, enjoy positions which call on him to travel
a lot – thereby disrupting his ordered lifestyle – and his direct
and matter-of-fact manner may work against him in positions
which involve selling. If given a choice, the Ox often prefers to
work on his own rather than with others.

The Ox is also careful in financial matters. He looks after his
money well and tends to have simple rather than expensive
tastes. Through shrewd financial planning, most Oxen are financially secure in later life. However, while the Ox is restrained in
his spending he can be most generous to his family and close
friends.

The Ox is very much a private person and often chooses to
keep himself to himself. He is not that great a socializer and may
have an aversion to large parties and social functions. He is also
not one for small talk and inane pleasantries and, in situations he
dislikes, the Ox can become introverted and even morose. The
Ox also does not have a particularly pronounced sense of
humour.

The Ox chooses his friends carefully and it often takes a long
time before he lets anyone into his confidence. Often he has a

small circle of close friends, frequently from his childhood years, and they are people who have earnt his respect and trust over a long period. The Ox is similarly careful in matters of the heart and is not one for quick romances. He may not be as demonstrative in his affections as some, but once he has chosen his partner he will remain loyal and faithful and fully aware of his responsibilities. However, while he will care deeply for his partner and seek to build up a stable and secure home life, he is not always an easy person to live with. He can be demanding, sets high standards and likes to have his own way. He also likes to plan, organize and dominate his household and will make sure his home is run in an efficient and orderly manner.

The Ox is also conscientious in his role as a parent. He will be firm but fair and will make sure his children have a sound and thorough education. He will encourage them as much as he can and will do much to ensure they have a secure environment in which to develop. The Ox sets a fine example for his children to follow.

The lady Ox is a practical person. Like all Oxen, she organizes her activities with great care. She is keenly aware of her responsibilities and is supportive to her partner and her children. She also takes much delight in maintaining her home and others often marvel at her industry and capabilities. She is direct and friendly in her manner and can be quite ambitious. In dress, she often prefers simple but practical outfits.

The male Ox is quiet but confident in his manner. He may not be as outgoing as other signs, but he has a sharp mind and a steely resolve. His calm and placid exterior often conceals a strong ambitious nature.

The Ox has many fine and distinctive qualities. He works hard, is reliable and honourable in his dealings. He never promises more than he can deliver and with his confident and no-nonsense manner, is often a source of inspiration for others. However, the Ox does have his weaknesses. He can be stubborn and intransigent and does not adapt well to change. He also tends to rely so much on his abilities that he is not always mindful of the views and feelings of those around him. He can be prejudiced, inflexible and intolerant. He is also not a good loser and if things go against him the Ox can become bitter and resentful. He also has an awesome temper, although fortunately it is only used on rare occasions. However, at all times, the Ox is keenly aware of his responsibiliti ›s and while he may appear to be private and rather aloof, he will be respected and admired by many. His sincerity, honesty and integrity is appreciated by all who know him.

The Ox's life is often one of steady progress. With his set interests and tendency to specialize, the Ox's persistence and tenacity will eventually lead him to his goals.

As a child the Ox likes to keep himself to himself and sets about his endeavours and school work in a responsible and disciplined way. He is well-intentioned and strives to please, although at times he can be stubborn and obstinate and this will lead to inevitable conflict with parents and teachers. The Ox is, however, usually a quiet child and, although he may not always show it, he very much values the love and attention of his parents.

As the Ox matures he often devotes much time and energy to his studies and will usually become proficient in a specialist area. His work may bring him much satisfaction but, being so reserved by nature, he may not always feel at ease with matters of the heart.

Once the Ox settles down, he will be keen to do well and make the most of his abilities, but there is a danger that he can get so preoccupied with his own concerns that he is not always mindful of the feelings of those around him. Without care, this can cause problems for the Ox and give rise to difficulties as middle age approaches.

In later life the Ox can look forward to reaping the rewards of his efforts and many will make their mark in their chosen profession and enjoy a secure, stable and comfortable way of life.

Old age is often a time of contentment for the Ox and he will take much delight in following the activities of his family as well as devoting himself to his own interests.

Henry David Thoreau, the American essayist and poet, was born under the sign of the Ox. He wrote, 'I know of no more encouraging fact than the unquestionable ability of man to elevate his life by conscious endeavour.' And the Ox's life is indeed one of conscious endeavour. Through his efforts, his abilities and persistence, his life will be worthy, satisfying and fulfilling.

Famous Oxen

Johann Sebastian Bach, Warren Beatty, Jon Bon Jovi, Jeff Bridges, King Carlos of Spain, Barbara Cartland, Charlie Chaplin, Natalie Cole, Bill Cosby, Tom Courtenay, Tony Curtis, Walt Disney, Patrick Duffy, Jane Fonda, Gerald Ford, Edward Fox, Michael J. Fox, Peter Gabriel, Richard Gere, Whoopi Goldberg, Mariel Hemingway, Robert Hardy, Nigel Havers, Dustin Hoffman, Anthony Hopkins, Billy Joel, Don Johnson, B. B. King, Mark Knopfler, Burt Lancaster, Jessica Lange, Angela Lansbury, Jack Lemmon, Alison Moyet, Eddie Murphy, Napoleon, Paul Newman, Jack Nicholson, Robert Redford, Sissy Spacek, Bruce Springsteen, Rod Steiger, Meryl Streep, Elaine Stritch, Loretta Swit, Mary Tyler Moore, Lady Thatcher, Twiggy, Dick Van Dyke, the Princess of Wales, Zoe Wanamaker, Barbara Windsor.

The Tiger

Key characteristics: Bold, asserti e, adventurous, strong willed, independent, inventive, versatile, generous, sincere, well meaning but restless and impulsive.

In love: Sincere, passionate and a true romantic!

Proud, distinctive and ever alert, the tiger is a majestic animal. Governed by courage, he is a creature who is much admired and, similarly, those born under the third of the Chinese signs are just as distinguished. They are bold, enterprising and have little trouble in gaining the respect of others.

The Tiger has a lively nature. He likes to keep himself active and often has a wide range of interests. He has an inquisitive mind and is capable of much original thought. He is also bold in his actions and not averse to taking risks. He follows the courage of his convictions and many admire him for his sincere, resolute and courageous manner. The Tiger is open in expressing his views and cannot tolerate falsehood or hypocrisy. He is honest, possesses much integrity and has a warm and generous nature.

The Tiger often holds firm opinions and beliefs and while he might dispense advice to others, he rarely listens to that given to him. He relies on his own instinct and intuition. In many ways the Tiger is his own master and he likes to retain a certain independence in his actions.

With his enthusiasm, energy and determined nature the Tiger will often rise to the top of his chosen profession. He has considerable powers of leadership and enjoys positions of authority. The Tiger can be innovative in his business dealings and is capable of coming up with many excellent ideas. He also enjoys challenges and using his initiative, but can quickly become bored when faced with bureaucratic and routine matters. The Tiger can do well in commerce, marketing, politics, the police or military life, or in the media. He enjoys the limelight and his vitality and sheer strength of character make him someone to be noticed. The Tiger can often be a source of inspiration for others.

The Tiger has considerable earning abilities and is usually materially well off. However, he is not particularly materialistic in nature and spends his money quite freely. He can be extremely generous and takes delight in buying presents and treats for others. He also has a caring nature, is often interested in humanitarian matters and keen to support charities and help those less fortunate than himself. The Tiger is genuinely interested in others and has a kindly and well-meaning nature.

With his many interests, the Tiger is not one for spending long periods at home, but he will always make sure his home is comfortable and well equipped. He has a good eye for decoration and home furnishing. Also, in the early part of his life, the Tiger tends to move house quite frequently.

Although the Tiger cherishes his independence, he is a keen socializer and enjoys attending – and hosting – parties and functions. He will always maintain a wide circle of friends and, with his lively and often witty manner, is invariably popular.

In love, the Tiger is a romantic. He is sincere and open in his affections and has a passionate nature. He loves to love and be loved. When in love, the Tiger will devote himself entirely to the person of his affection and his feelings and passion will be intense. However, he does have a restless nature and in time his feelings may begin to wane and his attention begin to wander; his youth will often be characterized by many different romances. When he decides to settle down, however – and the Tiger often marries young – he will be loyal and faithful and most attentive to his partner. In return, the Tiger likes to play the dominant role in his marriage. He likes to have his own way but also to be able to go off and pursue his own interests. Even though he may be committed to his partner, he still craves for a certain freedom and if this is ever denied him, he can become restless and resentful.

The female Tiger has a warm and friendly nature. She is outgoing, has a sharp and alert mind and is often highly talented. She is ambitious and is greatly admired for her determined and versatile nature. She is also conscientious in her duties and is attentive to the needs of her partner and children. In particular, the Tigress takes an active interest in the education of her children and makes an admirable teacher.

Both the male and female Tiger pay much attention to their appearance. They like to be noticed and impress and often wear smart, elegant and fashionable clothes.

The Tiger has an attractive and vibrant personality. He is bold, adventurous and original. However, while he possesses many fine gifts, the Tiger also has his weaknesses. In his desire to get things done he can be impatient, impulsive and sometimes even reckless. In addition, he does not always persist in his activities and an initial burst of enthusiasm can soon evaporate if something more interesting captures his attention. He can be stubborn and obstinate and does not always heed advice. Naturally such an attitude will bring him into conflict with others and this in turn can give rise to a certain instability in his life. However, the Tiger is resourceful and resilient and even though he may face problems and obstacles in his life, he will invariably come bounding back with renewed energy and vigour. The Tiger is a dynamic figure who can never be ignored or underestimated.

At some time during his life the Tiger may be tempted to throw caution to the wind and go off and do what he wants to do. Whether it is to drop out of society for a time, travel round the world or abandon his job to fulfil an ambition, the Tiger is a risk taker and a law unto himself. He has a fine and adventurous spirit, living and enjoying life to the full.

The Tiger's life is often eventful and, as a child, he delights in the opportunities and challenges around him. He is forever learning new skills and feats and is full of energy, vitality and enthusiasm. He is quick to learn and has a wide range of interests. However, even at an early age, the Tiger does not like to obey and many a time his strong-mindedness will lead him into conflict with his parents and teachers. The Tiger child needs discipline and careful guidance, ut he is warm and loving in his affections.

With his independent nature, the Tiger is often eager to break free from parental authority and tends to leave home at an early age. His early adult years can prove a difficult time for him when he is keen to achieve much and prove himself to the world, but his impatience and lack of experience can lead to disappointment and frustration. He may also feel unsure how best to use his talents and in early adulthood he may be tempted to change his job – and his residence – fairly frequently.

As the Tiger matures, it is hoped he has learnt from his earlier experiences, is able to quell his restless spirit and persist in his activities. If so, the Tiger can enjoy considerable success and make his mark in his chosen profession. He has the skills and talents to do well and once he has the self-discipline, he will truly come into his own.

In old age the Tiger is able to look back on his life with much pride and satisfaction. Over the years he will have achieved and accomplished a great deal and will still delight in pursuing a wide range of activities as well as enjoying the company of those around him.

The Tiger life is often rich and rewarding and as the poet John Masefield, himself a Tiger, wrote

Most roads lead men homewards,
My road leads me forth.

The bold, adventurous and courageous Tiger is one who is always going forth.

Famous Tigers

Sir David Attenborough, Queen Beatrix of the Netherlands, Beethoven, Tony Bennett, Chuck Berry, Richard Branson, Garth Brooks, Mel Brooks, Agatha Christie, Phil Collins, Jason Connery, Gemma Craven, Tom Cruise, Emily Dickinson, Roberta Flack, Jodie Foster, Connie Francis, Crystal Gayle, Susan George, Elliott Gould, Buddy Greco, William Hurt, Derek Jacobi, Dorothy Lamour, Stan Laurel, Marilyn Monroe, Demi Moore, The Queen, Oliver Reed, Lionel Richie, Diana Rigg, Kenny Rogers, The Princess Royal, Sir Jimmy Savile, Phillip Schofield, Pamela Stephenson, Dame Joan Sutherland, Dylan Thomas, Liv Ullman, John Voigt, Julie Walters, Oscar Wilde, Tennessee Williams, Terry Wogan, Stevie Wonder.

THE RABBIT

Key characteristics: Sociabl . discreet, tactful, refined, peaceloving, careful, shrewd, perceptive, prudent, but sensitive and sometimes aloof.

In love: Romantic, passionate and a good judge of character.

Whether living among rolling downs, in lush meadows or fields, the rabbit appears a calm, peaceful and contented animal. And these attributes are found in many people born under the fourth Chinese sign.

The Rabbit is governed by virtue and prudence and has a quiet, refined and sociable manner. He prefers the quieter things in life and sets about his activities in a methodical and unflustered way. Intelligent, widely read and articulate, the Rabbit knows how to impress and will never be without friends.

The Rabbit is a companionable sign and relates well to others. He has a discreet and amiable manner and is both an eloquent speaker and good listener. He enjoys conversation and he often dispenses wise and shrewd advice. He also has a perceptive nature and is a good judge of character.

The Rabbit usually has a happy and contented disposition. He dislikes arguments and emotional scenes and will do his utmost to avoid any sort of unpleasantness. For the Rabbit, life is to be savoured and enjoyed and he sometimes shuts himself off from some of the harsher aspects of life. However, while he may take great pains to avoid difficult and contentious situations, if he has no alternative he will defend himself as well as anyone else.

In addition to enjoying conversation, the Rabbit can be a keen reader and has a fond appreciation of music, the arts and the countryside. Where possible he will try to live in pleasant and agreeable surroundings. He will furnish his home in fine style and has a good eye for decoration, furniture and accessories. Many Rabbits are also collectors and have a penchant for antiques, *objets d'art* and paintings.

The Rabbit is a creature of comfort and likes to maintain a high standard of living. He enjoys socializing, attending parties and functions, and also takes delight in entertaining his many friends. He makes a superb and attentive host.

With his careful and methodical nature, the Rabbit often does well in his work. He is an astute businessperson, ever alert and watchful, and has good judgement. He can also be cunning in his actions and is a shrewd and skilful negotiator. With his quiet and genial manner he experiences little difficulty in winning the support of others, although his desire to avoid confrontation sometimes makes him err on the side of caution. With his intellect, good memory and eye for detail the Rabbit is often well suited to an administrative or academic career. He also makes a fine diplomat and can do well in PR work, the law, in the financial sector or in some aspect of the arts. He may also make an astute antique dealer. Ideally the Rabbit will choose to specialize in one career rather than switching from one occupation to another and he will also do much to avoid working in a particularly fraught or frenzied atmosphere.

The Rabbit tends to deliberate long and hard in his activities and is seldom given to rash or impulsive actions. He attaches great importance to his security and is careful and prudent in money matters. He is often a shrewd investor and most Rabbits are financially secure in later life.

Both male and female Rabbits take much pride in their appearance and choose smart and stylish clothes. The female Rabbit carries herself with much dignity and is often an elegant woman. She is softly spoken and has an affectionate and kindly nature. She frequently has a circle of close friends and is greatly admired for her discretion and understanding. She may be quiet in manner but she has a delicious sense of fun and knows what she wants in life.

The male Rabbit is also popular. Often good looking, he has considerable charm and his quiet and agreeable manner will win him many friends and supporters.

Being sociable, both male and female Rabbits attach much importance to their relations with others. The Rabbit has a romantic and passionate nature and is likely to have many romances before settling down. He is a good judge of character and usually makes a fine choice of partner. Generally, most Rabbits are loyal and faithful but there are a few who cannot quell their flirtatious natures and indulge in extra-marital affairs.

With their partner the Rabbit will take much pleasure in establishing a secure, comfortable and cosy home. The Rabbit makes a fine homemaker and will invariably keep his home tidy and well organized. Rabbits tend to have large families although the responsibilities of parenthood do not always come easily. Although he will love and care for his children dearly, some Rabbits find children a disruptive influence on their otherwise orderly lifestyle and have difficulty in coping with their more boisterous antics. However, children do generally relate well to his kindly and affectionate manner and the Rabbit will always do his best to make sure his children are well provided for and support them in their activities.

The Rabbit has considerable qualities. He is well mannered and tactful. He has a keen intellect, is conscientious in his work and has refined and cultured tastes. However, he also has his weaknesses – he can be over-sensitive and his desire to avoid problems and difficulties can make him hesitant and faint-hearted. If things are not to his liking he can become distant and aloof and, sometimes, to get round situations, he can be rather superficial in his attitude. He can also be fussy and pedantic. However, his astute, perceptive and careful nature usually enables him to steer a safe course. As far as possible he will lead an agreeable and pleasant life; a life spent enjoying the company of others and pursuing his various interests.

The different stages of the Rabbit's life can bring him content-ment and pleasure although much is dependent on him feeling secure and at ease with himself and his surroundings. Stability and security are all-important to him and should anything calamitous occur or major difficulties arise, then his whole being may be sent into a turmoil from which he may take some time to recover.

As a child, the Rabbit will be well behaved, compliant and eager to please. He learns well and may excel in academic subjects. However, the Rabbit child can be sensitive and acutely aware of the feelings of others and this sensitivity can, at times, cause him much anguish.

With his sociable nature the Rabbit will enjoy his youth and early adulthood. This will be a time of great romance, much socializing and a time when he will decide upon his career and the direction of his life – and the Rabbit often chooses wisely. As the Rabbit matures, he will strive to build up a settled home and enjoy a comfortable lifestyle.

In old age, some Rabbits tend to withdraw into themselves and can become more solitary in nature. However, the Rabbit will be able to look back on his many achievements and at the happy times he has enjoyed as well as the happiness he has brought to others.

Thomas Carlyle, the historian, was a Rabbit and he once wrote, 'The man without a purpose is like a ship without a rudder.' The Rabbit will never be like a rudderless ship. He has a definite purpose in life – to live it and enjoy it to the full – and in this, the Rabbit usually succeeds admirably.

Famous Rabbits

Prince Albert, Lucy Arnaz, Harry Belafonte, Ingrid Bergman, James Caan, Lewis Carroll, John Cleese, Confucius, Albert Einstein, Peter Falk, W. C. Fields, Peter Fonda, James Fox, Sir David Frost, James Galway, Cary Grant, Edvard Grieg, Oliver Hardy, Paul Hogan, Bob Hope, Whitney Houston, John Hurt, David Jason, Michael Keaton, John Keats, Cheryl Ladd, Danny La Rue, Julian Lennon, Patrick Lichfield, Gina Lollobrigida, Ali MacGraw, George Michael, Roger Moore, Nanette Newman, Tatum O'Neal, Christina Onassis, Ken Russell, Mort Sahl, Elizabeth Schwarzkopf, George C. Scott, Neil Sedaka, Jane Seymour, Neil Simon, Frank Sinatra, Dusty Springfield, Sting, Jimmy Tarbuck, Tina Turner, Luther Vandross, Queen Victoria, Andy Warhol, Orson Welles.

THE DRAGON

Key characteristics: Active, alert, determined, confident, enterprising, versatile, forthright, resilient, scrupulous, impulsive and lucky.

In love: Passionate, faithful and sincere – but can be demanding!

Flamboyant, colourful and vibrant, the dragon makes a splendid leader of the carnival. He is a creature of awe, of mystique and power. He has charisma, vitality and energy. And so, too, do many people born under the fifth Chinese sign.

The Dragon is governed by luck and has a lively and outgoing nature. He has a quick and alert mind and is possessed with much energy and enthusiasm. Once the Dragon has an idea – and he has them in plenty – he will let nothing stand in his way until he has achieved his objective. He is a doer and an achiever, and has a most determined nature. And this zest, enthusiasm and energy are highly infectious. He can enthuse others with his projects and plans and often has little difficulty in winning the support and approval of those around him. With his confident and self-assured manner he has considerable leadership qualities. He has the courage of his convictions and is often prepared to take risks in order to obtain what he wants. Many times the Dragon is successful, but he can also be impulsive and impatient and does not always pay sufficient attention to detail. But even if his plans do not work exactly as he had hoped, his resilience and faith keep him going and he will seek out new opportunities to pursue. The Dragon thrives on challenges and is constantly setting himself new goals and objectives. It has been said that the

27

Dragon does not recognize the word 'impossible' and with his tremendous will-power and self-belief, more times than not he will achieve what he wants.

With his sharp mind and sense of determination the Dragon often rises to the top of his chosen profession. As he is so skilled and versatile, this can be in almost any area he chooses. However, the Dragon enjoys pⁱ sitions of authority and situations where he can use his initiative. He often does well in business, commerce, politics, the performing arts and in positions which allow him to indulge in his love of travel. With his energetic and often athletic nature, Dragons can also excel in sport. However, they should avoid positions which involve a lot of routine – without variety or challenge the Dragon can soon become restless and bored.

The Dragon is also scrupulously fair in his dealings with others. He is open and honest and despises any sort of hypocrisy and falsehood. Occasionally, however, he is too trusting and there will be times when he could find himself having been duped by those less scrupulous than himself. When this occurs, those responsible will be sure to regret their actions. The wrath of an angered Dragon can be great indeed! The Dragon is also very direct in his dealings with others. He can be forthright in expressing his views and is certainly no diplomat. He can also be demanding and expects those around him to follow his own high example.

Exuberant and confident, the Dragon tends to be at the forefront of whatever he is doing. To some extent he is a showman and he likes to be noticed and win the approval of others. Similarly, in matters of the heart he will never be short of admirers. He has style, grace and allure and with his lively and sociable nature he makes fascinating company. He has an amorous and passionate nature and will often enjoy many romances. However, in spite of his popularity and appeal, matters of the heart do not always go smoothly for the Dragon. The Dragon has a strong independent streak in him and he may find it difficult to sacrifice this independence for another person. Although Dragons enjoy being married, there are others who are just as happy remaining single and cherishing the independence to do as they please.

However, when the Dragon chooses to marry he likes to play the dominant role in his marriage. He does not acquiesce easily and he likes to have his own way. He is, though, loyal and supportive to his partner, keenly aware of his responsibilities and strives to establish a secure and stable home. However, he is not one who tolerates emotional scenes or upsets and, being so self-sufficient, does not always fully understand or appreciate the worries and concerns of others. For the more sensitive, the Dragon's attitude – even though it may be unintentional – can be hurtful.

If he has children the Dragon can be a firm but loving parent. He will be quick to spot where his children's talents lie and will do much to encourage and support them. However, he does have high expectations for them and sets high standards. He also expects to be obeyed and woe betide any children who flout his authority or incur his wrath. The Dragon can be a hard task-master but many children will benefit from his discipline, his love and expert guidance.

The female Dragon is versatile and highly gifted. She is ambitious and confident and knows what she wants in life. She also has a great deal of determination and once she has set her mind on a certain goal she will not rest until she has reached it. The female Dragon is an immensely practical person and is much loved and respected by those around her. She is popular, will have many friends and carries herself with considerable aplomb. The female Dragon often chooses simple clothes and tends not to use too much make-up, if any. She prefers to let her natural and often considerable beauty speak for itself.

The male Dragon is self-assured in his manner and keen to make the most of his abilities. He often has an athletic build and keeps himself fit with an active and energetic lifestyle.

With his skills and enterprising nature the Dragon has considerable earning abilities. However, while he is not particularly materialistic in outlook, he enjoys spending money on himself, his family and his friends. He also likes to lead an active social life and enjoys travel.

The Dragon has many fine qualities, but also has faults. In his desire to get things done he car be reckless and impulsive. He can also be stubborn and while he often dispenses good advice to others, he does not always take heed of advice given to him. He can be demanding and intolerant, but is sincere and honourable in his manner. He works hard and is resourceful and diligent. He commands respect and admiration and his faith and belief in himself help him through both good and bad times.

The different phases of the Dragon's life are often quite distinct. Childhood for the Dragon can be both a wonderful but difficult time. The Dragon child is intelligent, quick to learn and gifted in many different areas. He enjoys the challenges he is given and relishes the opportunities that are around him. However, he can also be stubborn and independent-minded and this can lead him into conflict with others. Although he may be high-spirited and not always the easiest to discipline, with his many gifts he will often be a source of much pride to his parents.

The Dragon's youth and early adulthood may be a tricky time for him. The Dragon is keen to prove himself and to realize his potential, though sometimes he can be unrealistic in his expectations or try to achieve too much too soon. His impatience and impulsive manner can lead to disappointments and he may need to reconcile his hopes and aspirations to the real world. While at this time not all his plans may come to fruition, he nevertheless delights in his independence and responsibilities and revels in the challenges and opportunities that lie before him. He also enjoys the fruits of love and with his attractive looks and striking personality has no shortage of admirers. Whether married or single, the relations that the Dragon establishes at this time will bring him much happiness. The Dragon usually chooses his partner and friends well.

As the Dragon matures and settles down, his talents and abilities will be recognized and he can enjoy considerable success. The final phase of his life, too, will bring him much happiness. He will be able to reflect on his many achievements as well as enjoy the material comforts around him. His life will be full and eventful and he will have much ɔ look back on with pride and satisfaction.

The playwright George Bernard Shaw was a Dragon and he once declared, 'The people who get on in this world are the people who get up and look for the circumstances they want, and if they cannot find them, make them.' His words apply to many born under this most enterprising and vibrant sign. The Dragon is a doer and an achiever, and throughout his life he will also be blessed with much luck.

Famous Dragons

Jenny Agutter, Jeffrey Archer, Roseanne Arnold, Joan Baez, Count Basie, Neneh Cherry, Julie Christie, James Coburn, Bing Crosby, Salvador Dali, Charles Darwin, Susan Dey, Neil Diamond, Matt Dillon, Christian Dior, Fats Domino, Placido Domingo, Faye Dunaway, Prince Edward, Adam Faith, Bruce Forsyth, James Garner, Che Guevara, David Hasselhoff, Tom Jones, Eartha Kitt, John Lennon, Abraham Lincoln, Lee Majors, Francois Mitterrand, Bob Monkhouse, Florence Nightingale, Al Pacino, Elaine Paige, Gregory Peck, Richard Pryor, Christopher Reeve, Cliff Richard, Mel Smith, Ringo Starr, Princess Stephanie of Monaco, Mr T, Shirley Temple, Raquel Welch, Mae West, Frank Zappa.

THE SNAKE

Key characteristics: Thoughtful, reflective, wise, shrewd, intuitive, placid, guarded, independent, cautious, but sometimes lazy.

In love: Passionate, seductive and most possessive!

Whether slithering through long undergrowth or lying coiled under some rock, the snake is a creature to be treated with care and respect. Silent, alert and ever watchful, the Snake is the sixth member of the Chinese zodiac.

The Snake is governed by wisdom and has a sharp and penetrating mind. He has a powerful intellect, is widely read and is a deep thinker. The Snake has an enquiring nature and a wide range of interests. Subjects such as religion, philosophy, politics, science and new beliefs often intrigue the Snake, as do some of the mysteries in life, such as strange phenomena and psychic matters.

The Snake has a quiet and reserved temperament. He chooses his friends with care and does not willingly let others into his confidence. He can be secretive and guarded and in many matters chooses to be his own master. The Snake relies a lot on his own perception and intuition and does not always listen to the advice of others. Some may find his manner cool and evasive but should they try to penetrate through the Snake reserve they will discover a rich, warm and gentle character.

The Snake is often softly spoken and some, particularly in their early years, may not be good communicators, but the Snake generally speaks carefully and wisely. Many pay great heed to the words of a Snake and his views and opinions are often sought and respected. The Snake is also not one for small talk, but he does possess a good sense of humour.

With his powerful intellect, the Snake can often do well in his chosen career. He has a sharp incisive mind and good judgement. He is best suited to more cerebral occupations and often succeeds in careers such as teac'ing, politics, writing, science, the law, stockbroking and even astrology. The Snake does not enjoy manual labour.

Ideally the Snake prefers to take his time in conducting his various activities. He hates being hurried or hassled into taking quick decisions and likes to plan his work carefully. He is an effective organizer and uses his time wisely. When he has a particular objective that he wishes to attain, he will let nothing stand in his way until he has secured what he wants. When motivated, the Snake can be relentless in pursuing his goals. However, should adversity strike and his plans fail, it can prove a devastating experience. The Snake is a poor loser, takes failure badly and it often takes him a long time to recover from setbacks.

The Snake is also adept in handling financial matters. He is an astute investor and looks after his finances well. He spends his money carefully but if there is something that he wants, he will not rest until it is his. What the Snake wants, he usually gets. The Snake prefers not to lend to others and can appear tightfisted to some, though he can be most generous to those close to him. With their financial skills and usual good fortune, most Snakes are financially secure in old age. However, despite his financial acumen, the Snake should avoid gambling. The Snake has the distinction of being the unluckiest gambler in the Chinese zodiac. Snakes, be warned!

By being so watchful and having such a determined nature, the Snake tends to burn up much nervous energy and can sometimes be prone to nervous disorders. However, once they have secured their objectives, many Snakes are often happy to sit back and enjoy the fruits of their labours. Frequently, after a bout of activity and exertion, the Snake finds it necessary to rest and unwind and restore lost energy. He might have the determination to secure his objectives, but not always the stamina. Also the Snake does have a slight streak of laziness in him and if he sees a short cut or thinks he can get away without doing something, he is sure to try.

The Snake does, however, take great care over his appearance and the female Snake carries herself with style and grace. She takes care in choosing her clothes and often adorns herself with beautiful jewellery. She is highly attractive and has a quiet, confident and enchanting manner. The male Snake, too, prides himself on his appearance and carries himself with considerable dignity. Both the male and female Snake have good taste and make the most of themselves and their good looks.

With his wide interests, quiet manner and good humour, the Snake exudes an almost irresistible charm. He is romantic, seductive and passionate – almost the Don Juan of the Chinese signs – and he does not lack for admirers. However, once the Snake has fallen in love he can be possessive. He demands total loyalty and faithfulness from his partner and if he has any grounds for jealousy he takes it very much to heart. For some the Snake's possessiveness may become too overbearing, but many enjoy the love, affection and security that the Snake gives. The Snake has a powerful sexual instinct and is one of the most seductive of the Chinese signs.

Ideally the Snake should not marry too young. He has a flirtatious nature and it is often best for him to enjoy the freedom of youth before settling down to married life. Even though he demands the total loyalty of his partner, there are some Snakes who cannot control their flirtatious nature and indulge in extra-marital affairs. In matters of morality, some Snakes can be hypocrites.

The Snake places great value on his home and strives to make it comfortable and furnish it in good taste. As with most things, the Snake makes sure his home is outwardly pleasing even though the cupboards and drawers may be crammed with his many knick-knacks and possessions. Also, in his home, he tries to establish a calm and stable atmosphere – the Snake does not like undue noise or to live in a whirl of frenzied activity. A peaceful, leisurely and comfortable existence is what the Snake craves for, and usually achieves.

The Snake makes a loving parent and will care deeply for his children. With his wide interests, quiet considerate manner and delicious sense of fun, he relates well to children and can establish a good rapport with them. The Snake parent may, however, have problems over discipline. He is not one who copes well with domestic scenes or childhood upsets.

The different phases in the Snake's life are quite separate. As a child, the Snake has a quiet and reserved nature. He often prefers his own company and takes great delight in amusing himself with his many imaginative games. At school the Snake can be a late developer and throughout his early years he needs all the love and guidance that his parents can give. Although he enjoys being left to his own devices, he can still be demanding of his parents and likes to secure his parents' exclusive attention. Even in his early years the Snake's possessive streak will be evident.

The Snake's youth may prove difficult as he faces the world and his new responsibilities for the first time and grapples with his emotions, romance and then the demands of family life. Often it is not until his late twenties or thirties that the Snake finally feels able to settle down and decide upon the direction of his life. Then there will be no stopping him and he will relentlessly pursue his goals and aspirations, often achieving success.

The Snake's more mature years will be spent enjoying the fruits of his labours. Most Snakes are materially well off in old age and this is when the Snake will settle back and indulge in his interests and memories.

The Snake has a complex personality. Wise, alert, refined and reserved, the Snake is his own man. But behind this there lurks serenity, gentleness, good humour and powerful sensuality. The Snake has much to offer and throughout his life he will endeavour to give of his best and make the most of his considerable abilities. The German writer Johann Wolfgang von Goethe was a Snake and he once wrote, 'Just trust yourself, then you will know how to live.' And the Snake, with his quiet and intuitive nature, is a person who very much trusts himself.

Famous Snakes

Muhammad Ali, Ann-Margret, Kim Basinger, Tony Blair, Pierce Brosnan, Tom Conti, Randy Crawford, Jim Davidson, Bob Dylan, Henry Fonda, Mahatma Gandhi, Greta Garbo, Art Garfunkel, Dizzy Gillespie, Stacy Keach, Howard Keel, J. F. Kennedy, Carole King, James Last, Dame Vera Lynn, Linda McCartney, Mao Tse-tung, Nigel Mansell, Dean Martin, Robert Mitchum, Bob Newhart, Ryan O'Neal, Dorothy Parker, Pablo Picasso, Mary Pickford, Andre Previn, Helen Reddy, Griff Rhys-Jones, Franklin D. Roosevelt, Mickey Rourke, Franz Schubert, Brooke Shields, Paul Simon, Dionne Warwick, Charlie Watts, Ruby Wax, Oprah Winfrey, Virginia Woolf, Victoria Wood, Susannah York.

THE HORSE

Key characteristics: Active, alert, quick witted, outgoing, adventurous, eloquent, sociable, persuasive, restless, quick tempered and can be self-centred.

In love: To the Horse, love means everything. Passionate, attentive and faithful.

Over the centuries man has harnessed the skills and strengths of the horse in many different ways. From racing and riding to pulling carts, carriages and wagons, the horse has proved a versatile and adaptable animal. And this versatility is evident in those born under the sign of the Horse.

The Horse is quick witted, has a sharp mind and a wide range of interests. He has grace, style and elegance and throughout his life he will put his talents to many uses. He is adaptable, often restless and constantly thirsting for new challenges and things to do. The Horse has an adventurous spirit and likes to live life to the full.

The Horse has an amiable and engaging personality and makes friends with ease. He is a persuasive and eloquent speaker with a lively repartee. The Horse enjoys company and is a keen socializer. There is also something of a showman in the Horse – he enjoys the limelight and being the centre of attention. With his agreeable manner, his sharp mind and ready wit, he tends to dominate many of the activities with which he is associated. It is difficult to ignore a Horse and folly to do so.

The Horse has considerable powers of leadership and many rise to the top of their chosen profession. However, success for the Horse does not always come immediately. First he must conquer his restless spirit and in his early years he may try his hand at many different occupations before he finally decides what he wishes to do. The Horse also tends to lack persistence, and is easily distracted, which can delay his success. However, to make up for his failings, he sets about most of his undertakings with much zest and enthusiasm. He can work long and hard and, when motivated, is a splendid example to others. He is ambitious and competitive, and has considerable willpower. He also has a tremendous desire to succeed and to prove himself. The Horse is not one who takes failure well.

In his occupation the Horse seeks challenge and variety and enjoys working with others rather than on his own. With his engaging and persuasive personality, he can make an effective salesperson or politician and, with his practical nature, also do well as a technician, craftsman or doctor. He may also be attracted to positions which allow him to travel. With their energy and often athletic nature, Horses have also enjoyed much success in sport.

As he is versatile and adaptable, the Horse has considerable earning ability. However, providing he has sufficient funds to tide himself over, the Horse is not particularly concerned with the pursuit of wealth. He tends to spend any spare money he has freely and can be generous to others. A fair proportion of his money will be spent on socializing, entertaining and simply on enjoying himself.

The Horse's social life is very important to him and he will have friends and acquaintances in many walks of life. He relates well to others and is able to converse intelligently on a wide range of subjects. With his sense of fun and lively manner, other people enjoy his company. The Horse also exudes a strong sex appeal and both male and female Horses never lack for admirers. He has a passionate nature and when he is attracted to someone he devotes himself entirely to that person. His whole being is affected and the Horse is totally and utterly in love. The problem is that the Horse tends to fall in and out of love relatively easily and it takes someone special, someone who understands the Horse character well, to retain his affection. While life with the Horse can sometimes be demanding, it can also be exhilarating and the Horse makes a loyal and faithful partner.

The Horse often marries young and if he has children he is a firm parent, but does much to en ourage and stimulate his children's interests. Children like his lively nature and generally respond well to him.

The female Horse has a particularly engaging manner. She is versatile, has many interests (housework is not usually one of them, though!) and is a persuasive speaker. She has an adventurous and rather carefree spirit and a good sense of humour. She is intelligent, perceptive and popular. She is attractive in her looks and takes pride in her appearance. Often she chooses bright, colourful clothes and has poise, elegance and an irresistible charm.

The male Horse, too, cuts a dashing figure. Often good looking, he has style and a powerful and winning personality. Both male and female Horses carry themselves with dignity and pride.

The Horse has many fine qualities and is greatly admired and respected by others. However, the Horse's weaknesses can sometimes undermine his success. Above all, he is restless. He tends to jump from one activity to another and even abandon projects if something else catches his attention. If the Horse can overcome his restlessness and persevere more in his endeavours he may find life much easier. He can also let his enthusiastic nature get the better of him and can act impulsively or get carried away in the excitement of the moment. He has a quick temper and while he might later apologise for his outbursts, the damage could well have been done. He can at times be self-centred, over-talkative and temperamental but to offset this he is greatly admired for his integrity, honesty and sociable manner. The Horse has sparkle, wit and a zest for life and while he may not be the easiest person to live with, life with the Horse is certainly never boring.

The different phases of the Horse's life are often varied and distinct. His childhood years are full of wonder and excitement. The Horse child indulges in a wide range of interests and, with his great sense of fun, is popular with his peers. However, his boisterous and sometimes self-willed nature may bring him into conflict with both his parents and the authorities at school. He has a strong desire for independence and this causes many Horses to leave home at an early age. The Horse often marries young and his early adult years may be the most difficult. Independence, and the responsibilities it brings, can lead to disappointments, worry and burdens. At this time in his life the Horse is also trying to sort out what he wishes to do and achieve in life and, given his versatile nature, such a decision may not always be straightforward.

Life does, however, become easier as he matures. He learns from his early experiences and sets about his activities with a greater persistence and determination. He makes better use of his skills and talents and, with his diligence, ability for hard work and personable nature, he readily impresses others and makes the progress that may have eluded him in earlier years.

Old age is a time of contentment for the Horse. He has his family, his many friends and numerous interests and all are a great source of pleasure to him. If possible he also indulges his love of travel.

Every 60 years is the year of the Fire Horse. The last two Fire Horse years were 1906 and 1966 and the next is 2026. Those born in Fire Horse years often have the qualities (and weaknesses) of the Horse accentuated in their personality. The Fire Horse is blessed with much endurance and destined to lead an important and significant life.

The Horse is governed by elegance and ardour and is one of the more outgoing and energetic of the Chinese signs. He has charm, considerable appeal and a quick and sharp mind. The

American showman, P. T. Barnum, was a Horse and he once declared, 'Your success depends on what you do yourself, with your own means.' With his versatility and enterprise the Horse has considerable means and, once he has decided how best to use these means, his life can be rich and immensely fulfilling.

Famous Horses

Neil Armstrong, Rowan Atkinson, Cheryl Baker, Ingmar Bergman, Karen Black, Helena Bonham-Carter, Chopin, Sean Connery, Billy Connolly, Catherine Cookson, Ronnie Corbett, Elvis Costello, Kevin Costner, James Dean, Kirk Douglas, Clint Eastwood, Britt Ekland, Ella Fitzgerald, Harrison Ford, Aretha Franklin, Bob Geldof, Sally Gunnell, Gene Hackman, Susan Hampshire, Rolf Harris, Rita Hayworth, Jimi Hendrix, Janet Jackson, Dr Helmut Kohl, Lenin, Annie Lennox, Paul McCartney, Nelson Mandela, Princess Margaret, Spike Milligan, Ben Murphy, Stephanie Powers, Rembrandt, Barbra Streisand, Kiefer Sutherland, Patrick Swayze, John Travolta, Kathleen Turner, Vivaldi, Robert Wagner, Billy Wilder, Andy Williams, Tammy Wynette, Boris Yeltsin, Michael York.

THE GOAT

Key characteristics: Creative, imaginative, artistic, kindly, friendly, considerate, generous, easygoing, whimsical, sensitive, indecisive and a worrier.

In love: Amorous, affectionate and caring.

Whether grazing in a lush green field or gaily jumping over mountain rocks, the goat has an air of contentment about him, and so do many people born under the sign of the Goat.

Governed by art, the Goat possesses a rich imagination, is creative and prefers the quieter things in life. He has a kindly and caring nature and relates well to others. The Goat hates any sort of discord or unpleasantness and quickly shies away from arguments, disputes or awkward situations. Basically the Goat seeks a secure, comfortable and harmonious existence and when he has obtained all three he is truly content.

The Goat is, however, not as disciplined as some. Due to his relaxed and easygoing manner, he sometimes appears to drift and is not a particularly well-organized or punctual person. He also dislikes being bound by petty rules and regulations.

In his work the Goat needs an inspiring force behind him. Without this the Goat often lacks the motivation or drive to make the most of his abilities. However, once inspired the Goat can be a diligent and careful worker. He prefers to follow rather than lead and is not a risk-taker. He often chooses to concentrate on areas that interest him rather than become embroiled in awkward and potentially fraught situations. With his artistic skills the Goat excels in any position which enables him to use his creative or imaginative talents. Goats may also do well in the performing arts, in design and craft work and, with their love of nature, working with animals. Goats often have strong religious beliefs and can be drawn to careers in the Church or helping others through social work. The Goat tends not to be commercially minded and makes a poor salesman.

The Goat is generally fortunate in money matters and whether through luck, marriage or his own skills, he invariably has sufficient funds to live comfortably. However, the Goat enjoys spending money and has an acquisitive nature. Many Goats are collectors and find it hard to resist buying antiques, paintings or other objects of beauty for their home.

The Goat not only spends freely on himself but is generous to others and willingly gives to charity or helps those in need. Sometimes, however, the Goat can be gullible and there are some who take advantage of the Goat's kindly nature – here the Goat is in need of a mentor.

With his genial temperament, the Goat makes friends with ease and, although he may be shy and reserved on meeting someone for the first time, once he has got to know that person or feels confident in the group he is with, he can be talkative, witty and quite content to take centre stage. When the conditions are right the Goat comes into his own.

The Goat has a sincere and personable nature and enjoys the company of others. He dislikes solitude or loneliness and endeavours to have others around him. As regards his weaknesses, the Goat tends to worry a lot and can be a pessimist. But perhaps his greatest weakness is his capriciousness – the Goat is always changing his mind and his indecisiveness and hesitancy can often be an irritation for others. While those around the Goat may try to change him, rarely do they succeed. The Goat is born a capricious creature and invariably remains so all his life.

With such a friendly and sociable nature, the Goat values his relations with others and is invariably popular with the opposite sex. The Goat has a passionate and amorous nature and enjoys many romances. However, he can sometimes be reticent in expressing his true feelings and may experience much soul-searching before he finally decides to settle down. Whether this is due to the Goat's indecisiveness, his reluctance to take such a major step or some other factor, matters of the heart can cause the Goat much anxiety and emotional turmoil. Once settled, though, he is loving, loyal and most supportive to his partner.

The female Goat has a caring and considerate nature and is highly regarded by others. Admittedly she may not be the most organized of people, but she pours much love and energy into her family and home. She has good dress sense – often preferring ornate and pretty garments – and takes care with her appearance.

The male Goat, too, can look smart and presentable when he chooses but more often than not he will dress as he pleases – often casually and sometimes even to the point of scruffiness. He has a considerate and genial nature and while he may not be as assertive or competitive as some, his charm and persuasive nature can get him far.

The Goat often has a large family and makes a loving parent, but with his easygoing nature he is no disciplinarian and may not cope well with childhood scenes and tantrums. However, children respond well to the Goat's kindly nature and, with a few exceptions, Goat parents are able to establish a close and loving bond with their children.

The Goat's life progresses in distinct stages. As a child, the Goat seeks love and security and if his parents can provide this he will be content. Throughout his formative years he needs much support and gentle encouragement. Being so sensitive, he does not take criticism well and if he has difficulties at school or his homelife is unsettled, his confidence could be greatly undermined. He is, however, a generally obedient and affectionate child and while some Goats may opt to leave home early, the Goat always maintains close links with his parents.

The Goat's youth can prove a difficult time, finding he is often alone and fending for himself. There will be decisions to make and new and often daunting responsibilities and the Goat may find this an anxious and worrying time. Added to this will be the many romantic attachments he is likely to have and the soul-searching he is likely to go through before he finally settles down.

As the Goat matures and enjoys the support of his partner, his family or friends, he will begin to feel more secure and at ease. With the support and right encouragement behind him, the Goat will begin to realize and fulfil his potential and make more of his life. Old age will often be a contented time. His family, friends and his many memories will bring him much joy and, with his usual good fortune, he is materially well off and able to live comfortably.

The Goat is kindly and well meaning and seeks a quiet, settled and secure existence. He has a caring and considerate nature and throughout his life he brings pleasure to many and is much loved. As William Makepeace Thackeray, himself a Goat, declared, 'The world deals good-naturedly with good-natured people.' And the Goat certainly is good natured.

Famous Goats

Jane Austen, Anne Bancroft, Cilla Black, Elkie Brooks, Coco Chanel, Nat 'King' Cole, Catherine Deneuve, John Denver, Ken Dodd, Douglas Fairbanks, Mel Gibson, Paul Michael Glaser, Mikhail Gorbachev, Larry Hagman, George Harrison, Hulk Hogan, Isabelle Huppert, Julio Iglesias, Mick Jagger, Paul Keating, Ben Kingsley, Franz Liszt, John Major, Michelangelo, Joni Mitchell, Leonard Nimoy, Robert de Niro, Oliver North, Des O'Connor, Michael Palin, Keith Richards, William Shatner, Freddie Starr, Lana Turner, Mark Twain, Rudolph Valentino, Vangelis, Terry Venables, Lech Walesa, Barbara Walters, Andy Warhol, John Wayne, Tuesday Weld, Bruce Willis, Debra Winger.

The Monkey

Key characteristics: Resourceful, versatile, charming, persuasive, shrewd, amusing, sociable, likeable but lacks persistence and can be cunning.

In love: Captivating and knows how to impress!

The monkey has long held a fascination for mankind. Not only is this animal considered the closest to man, but his agility, energy and sense of fun make him appealing to watch. The monkey entertains and intrigues and those born under the Monkey sign are similarly skilled at capturing our attention and winning our approval. The Monkey is governed by fantasy, has a delightful sense of humour and a persuasive personality.

Indeed it is the Monkey's ability to get on well with others that helps him do so well in life. With his wit, charm and keen intellect the Monkey knows how to impress. He expresses himself well but he can also be crafty and cunning. If there is something that the Monkey wants he will use all the tricks in the book – and there will be many – to secure what he is after. The Monkey is immensely resourceful and is a supreme opportunist.

Along with his sociable and personable nature, the Monkey is highly intelligent. He has many interests and a most inquisitive nature. He enjoys reading, studying or finding out about things and he likes to keep himself well informed on a wide range of subjects. He also has an exceedingly good memory and many Monkeys excel in linguistics.

With his versatile and resourceful nature, the Monkey can do well in almost any line of work. However, he is probably at his best when facing challenges or has some objective to meet. He is a superb problem-solver and likes to use his initiative and abilities to the full. When faced with routine or mundane tasks the Monkey soon becomes bored. Generally, however, the Monkey does well in politics, marketing, industry, PR work or some aspect of the media, and with his strong imagination the Monkey makes a good writer and storyteller.

However, despite his diverse talents, the Monkey lacks persistence. If he feels something is going to take too long or a goal is not within immediate reach, his interest can soon wane. The Monkey is action oriented and is more interested in the present and the near future rather than years to come. In this respect his application and staying power can be weak. He needs variety and always has to have something to command his attention. He uses his time remarkably well and many marvel at just how much the Monkey can accomplish in a short space of time. When inspired and motivated, he has few equals.

The Monkey is shrewd in financial matters. He is adept at investing money or judging the profitability of any scheme. However, while he may be careful in money matters he may also be indulgent and never deprives himself of something that he may want. He can be generous to those close to him – or those he wants to impress – and, when it comes to his children, he will make sure that they want for nothing. The Monkey is also a keen traveller and is not averse to spending out on a lavish holiday or visiting distant parts of the world.

With his genial personality, the Monkey has many friends and makes good and interesting company. He has many interests and is versatile, so can talk intelligently on a wide range of subjects and relate to all manner of people. He is a skilful and persuasive speaker – although sometimes he can be just a little too talkative. With his retentive memory, he can remember interesting facts about people he has met and on a subsequent meeting will greatly impress them by remembering all manner of things about them. The Monkey knows how to impress – and he uses this skill to the utmost.

Having such a lively and engaging manner the Monkey is popular with the opposite sex, but affairs of the heart do not always run smoothly for this sign. There are several reasons for this. The Monkey, even though he may appear cheery and outgoing on the outside, is adept at hiding his true feelings and emotions. Others may think they know the Monkey but this is sometimes just a front he puts on. The Monkey does not willingly open up to others or let others into his confidence. He can be secretive and evasive and this caginess on the Monkey's part can cause him much emotional turmoil as well as undermining his relations with those close to him. It is certainly in his interests to be more open and trusting of others rather than be so guarded and mistrustful. The Monkey also has a tendency to be objective about his relationships and love, with all its emotion and complexity, does not always stand up to such scrutiny. Romance and love can, particularly in his youth, cause the Monkey much anguish. Often, however, the Monkey does marry young and, if possible, will choose to have a large family.

The Monkey truly delights in parenthood, particularly as it gives him the chance to rekindle the joys, delights and fun of his childhood years. The Monkey often remains young at heart and relates well to children, capturing their attention with his wit, imagination and intelligence.

The female Monkey has a lively and vivacious nature. Like her male counterpart, she is inquisitive, interested in all manner of subjects and is extremely versatile. She has a persuasive and engaging manner, likes to lead an active social life and has many friends. She is also ambitious and determined to make the best of her many talents. In appearance, she often chooses smart and fashionable clothes and likes to pay particular attention to her hair.

The male Monkey, too, tends to be smart in appearance. He likes to impress, not only with his personality but his looks – and he invariably succeeds.

The Monkey has many talents and with his resourceful attitude goes through life giving of his best and making the most of the opportunities that he sees. But he has his weaknesses. He can be vain, selfish and – if it is in his interests – cunning and crafty. He also has so much faith in his abilities that he does not always seek the support or advice of others and this can undermine his progress. In many ways the Monkey likes to remain his own man and he has a tendency to consider himself superior to others. However, while he has his faults, these are frequently concealed behind his friendly and likeable nature.

The Monkey invariably leads a fulfilling life, with each phase being marked by fresh challenges and opportunities. As a child the Monkey has numerous interests, is keen to learn and often has a great sense of fun and mischief. He is an adaptable and lively child and his childhood is often a time of wonder and contentment.

The Monkey's youth and early adulthood can be an exciting but anxious time for him. It is exciting because he is free to make his mark in the world and try out his many skills and ideas, but anxious because romance and matters of the heart can prove such a testing time for the Monkey. No longer can he hide behind his personable exterior but will need to relate, open up and trust another person and this does not always come easily to the Monkey.

In later adult life the Monkey immerses himself in his work and occupation, constantly seeking fresh challenges and opportunities. If, at any stage, his plans go wrong, he quickly learns from his mistakes and turns his attention to something new.

The Monkey does not, however, adapt so well to old age. Often he will have realized his ambitions and while he may still indulge in a wide range of interests and activities, his enthusiasm and zest may not be quite the same.

The philosopher Bertrand Russell was born under the sign of the Monkey and in true Monkey spirit, he declared, 'The secret of happiness is this: Let your interests be as wide as possible, and let your reactions to the things and persons that interest you be as far as possible friendly rather than hostile.' Russell's words hold good for many Monkeys. The Monkey is earnest, resourceful, adaptable and extremely likeable.

Famous Monkeys

Francesca Annis, Michael Aspel, Jacqueline Bisset, Julius Caesar, Princess Caroline of Monaco, Johnny Cash, Joe Cocker, Joan Crawford, Timothy Dalton, Bette Davis, Bo Derek, Jason Donovan, Michael Douglas, Mia Farrow, Carrie Fisher, Fiona Fullerton, Jerry Hall, Tom Hanks, Nigel Kennedy, Gladys Knight, Walter Matthau, Princess Michael of Kent, Kylie Minogue, Peter O'Toole, Robert Powell, Debbie Reynolds, Little Richard, Diana Ross, Boz Scaggs, Tom Selleck, Omar Sharif, Wilbur Smith, Koo Stark, Rod Stewart, Jacques Tati, Elizabeth Taylor, Dame Kiri Te Kanawa, Leonardo da Vinci.

THE ROOSTER

Key characteristics: Meticulous, methodical, efficient, orderly, conscientious, intelligent, honourable, trusting, well meaning, proud, but can be pedantic and notoriously candid.

In love: Sincere, caring and loyal.

Many a farm wakes up to the shrill cock-a-doodle-doo of a rooster. It is as if the rooster is the timekeeper, summoning everybody to rise and make the most of the day. Then, throughout the day, the rooster struts about proudly displaying his distinctive plumage, ever alert with his beady eyes. The rooster commands attention, is orderly and vigilant and so, too, are many who are born under the tenth Chinese sign.

Roosters are efficient and meticulous, organizing their activities with the utmost care. They are neat and tidy and have a great eye for detail. To some, the Rooster may appear fussy and pendantic, but the Rooster likes to get things right. He prides himself on his thoroughness and in many matters he is a perfectionist. One curious habit of the Rooster is that he invariably carries notebooks or scraps of paper around with him so that he can jot down reminders to himself or note down ideas. The Rooster is conscientious and cannot abide inefficiency.

The Rooster is also keenly intelligent. He has a sharp mind and remarkably good memory. He is often widely read and knowledgeable on a wide range of subjects. He is an adept and powerful speaker, enjoys discussion and if he knows he is going to be involved in some debate he will be sure to enter it fully prepared. A Rooster holding forth on some subject is an impressive sight. However, while the Rooster enjoys conversation and discourse, he is born under the sign of candour and this can make him forthright and frank when expressing his opinions. If he feels something needs to be said, the Rooster will say it. Some people greatly admire his honesty and forthrightness, but there are others who regard him as inconsiderate and abrasive.

In his manner the Rooster appears confident and self-assured. He is often given to flamboyant gestures and he likes to be in the limelight. He can be vain and tends to show off, but offsetting this he has an agreeable and friendly manner. He is sincere, honourable and trusting and can be fascinating company. The Rooster likes to lead an active social life. He is a keen party-goer and enjoys meals out or trips to the theatre or cinema. He likes to keep himself active and he lives life to the full. Extremely well-organized, it is sometimes remarkable at just what a Rooster can cram into a day, and, in addition to maintaining many diverse interests, he is often a keen traveller and gardener.

Those Roosters who are born between the hours of sunrise and sunset, 5–7a.m. and 5–7p.m., tend to be the more extrovert of their sign. These extroverts can indeed be particularly forceful and domineering characters, but there are other types of Rooster – particularly those born at night – who tend to be quieter and more reserved. Both extrovert and introvert Roosters carry themselves with pride and dignity and create an impression wherever they go. The whole demeanour of the Rooster, his manner, his gestures, and sometimes his appearance, make him someone to be noticed, someone who stands out from the crowd, someone with charisma.

With his intelligence, good eye for detail and his efficient manner, the Rooster can do well in his chosen career. He is meticulous in his work although in his desire to get things right he sometimes becomes so immersed in minor details that he wastes time on matters that are of little consequence. He also tends to be overambitious and sets himself unrealistic targets. Time after time a Rooster builds proverbial castles in the sky only to find his vision is unobtainable. However, despite this, the Rooster impresses others and with his skills, determination and shrewd mind he can obtain considerable success in his line of work. As he is so talented he is likely to try his hand at many different jobs before he finally settles on one particular career. With his active and outgoing nature the Rooster often excels in commerce, marketing or sales. He also makes a fine teacher and Roosters often enjoy uniformed positions, either in the police, the military services or in one of the public services. With his love of the land, the Rooster may also do well in farming and agriculture.

The Rooster has considerable earning ability but there are many Roosters – admittedly not all, but certainly a sizeable proportion – who tend to be great spendthrifts and find it hard to resist buying anything that catches their eye. The Rooster also has expensive tastes and invariably tries to buy the best. However, although the Rooster can be self-indulgent, he is also generous with his money and is often willing to help those less fortunate than himself or assist a friend in need.

As he is such a keen socializer, the Rooster has a wide circle of friends and acquaintances, and he is likely to have many romances before he settles down. Admittedly not all care for his forthright nature or exuberant manner, but he values his friend-ships and chooses his partner with care. The Rooster takes marriage seriously and in spite of a sometimes flirtatious youth, he is loyal and faithful to his partner. He is a good provider and makes sure that his home is orderly and run efficiently, prefer-ably to routine.

The Rooster may not be the easiest person to live with. He sets himself – and others – high standards and can be demanding and opinionated. However, underneath all the flamboyance and bluster there is a genuine, warm and extremely kindly person – a person who might not always be as confident as he may at first appear; a person who is anxious to do right, anxious to please. The Rooster has high moral viewpoints and conservative tastes, is sincere and capable of much love. However, it will take someone special to penetrate through the barriers that he sets up around himself. Although he may seem outgoing and highly sociable, he is in fact an intensely private person. He may gladly dispense advice to others but he keeps his own concerns strictly to himself and does not willingly let others into his confidence. Once his confidence has been won and the Rooster is prepared to lower his reserve though, you can be sure that he holds you in the highest esteem and, through good times and bad, will be a friend for life.

As a parent the Rooster can be strict, but caring. He makes sure his children do not want for anything and he is keen to guide them in their studies and interests. However, with his candid nature, the Rooster can sometimes upset a child's sensitivities and it would be in everyone's interest for him to exercise a little more thought before criticizing or admonishing a child too harshly. While the Rooster can be demanding and set his children high standards, his children will gain from the order and routine of a Rooster household. At least they know where they stand on any matter, what is or is not allowed and what is happening next.

The female Rooster, the Hen, is highly conscientious and thorough in all she does. In her work, the upbringing of her children or the upkeep of her home, she sets herself high standards and aims to please. She has a friendly and outgoing manner, and likes to lead an active social life as well as maintaining a multitude of often diverse interests. She chooses simple but good quality clothes and takes much care with her appearance. She has style, dignity and a most engaging manner.

The male Rooster likes to impress and tends to wear distinctive, sometimes ostentatious, clothes. He can, certainly in his youth, be outspoken and highly opinionated, and carries himself with considerable fortitude.

The Rooster's life may be full of ups and downs. There will be times when he will enjoy considerable success but other times when his plans and dreams do not materialize and he has to overcome disappointment and failure. However, his childhood is usually a happy time. He has an inquisitive nature and a wide range of interests and hobbies. He often does well at school and is a good learner. If he has brothers and sisters he will take great delight in helping, assisting and indeed organizing their activities as well. Even at an early age, the young Rooster is efficient and conscientious in his activities.

His youth, too, gives him much pleasure. He has a good circle of friends and with his outgoing and lively nature he is popular with the opposite sex. Romance, parties and an active social life find the Rooster in good form and enjoying life to the full. However, once the Rooster has settled down he will become keenly aware of his responsibilities. He aims to do his best, not only for his own satisfaction (and ego), but for those around him. Sometimes, however, his hopes and aspirations do not quite work out as he would like. In his early adult life he is constantly trying to improve himself and may possibly change his job quite often – sometimes with success, sometimes disappointment. But the Rooster is resilient and proud and his later adult life and old age will see him secure and content. The Rooster may not enjoy the luck of some and will need to work hard for his success, but he has many abilities and a determined nature. He is both a survivor and a winner.

Henry Ward Beecher, the American preacher, was a Rooster and he declared, 'A reputation for good judgement, for fair dealing, for truth, and for rectitude, is itself a fortune.' Many Roosters possess the qualities that make up the fortune.

Famous Roosters

Michael Caine, Enrico Caruso, Jasper Carrott, Christopher Cazenove, Eric Clapton, Joan Collins, Rita Coolidge, Sasha Distel, the Duke of Edinburgh, Gloria Estefan, Bryan Ferry, Errol Flynn, Dawn French, Stephen Fry, Steffi Graf, Melanie Griffith,

Richard Harris, Deborah Harry, Goldie Hawn, Katherine Hepburn, Diane Keaton, D. H. Lawrence, David Livingstone, Jayne Mansfield, Steve Martin, James Mason, Bette Middler, Van Morrison, Willie Nelson, Paul Nicholas, Kim Novak, Yoko Ono, Donny Osmond, Dolly Parton, Michelle Pfeiffer, Roman Polanski, Priscilla Presley, Nancy Reagan, Jenny Seagrove, Carly Simon, Jayne Torvill, Sir Peter Ustinov, Neil Young.

THE DOG

Key characteristics: Honest, trusting, dependable, diligent, direct, perceptive, selfless, altruistic, caring, but can be cynical and a pessimist.

In love: Very loyal and dutiful but keenly aware of the feelings of others.

Whether as a pet, a farm dog, a mountain rescuer or protector of property, the dog has long been regarded as man's best friend. Many of the noble features of the dog can be found in those born under this sign.

The Dog is governed by loyalty and anxiety. He has a dutiful and responsible manner and will stoutly defend what he believes is right. He is dependable, loyal and honourable and never promises more than he can deliver. He is a no-nonsense sort of person and hates any sort of pretentiousness, hypocrisy or falsehood.

The Dog is also a good judge of character. He takes his time in forming friendships and is much admired for his sincerity, good nature and integrity. The Dog inspires confidence and trust. He has a caring and altruistic nature and often lends his support to worthy and charitable causes. The Dog also has a strong sense of fair play and will stand up against injustice and wrongdoing and there have been many Dogs who have championed causes in which they fervently believe.

The Dog has a keen and alert mind and his diligence and loyalty is much appreciated by his employers. However to do well in his work, the Dog needs to feel inspired and motivated and consider that what he is doing is of benefit to others. If not, he may just drift and waste his many talents. Ideally the Dog is suited to jobs that serve and help others and he may do well in the medical profession, the church, politics, the law, teaching or social work. The Dog may not be as ambitious as some other signs but quite often he is elevated to positions of authority simply because he has earned the trust and confidence of others. Of all the Chinese signs, the Dog is one of the most selfless – his aim is to serve and to please.

With such a discreet, understanding and caring manner, the Dog is invariably popular and well liked. He chooses his friends with care and rarely lets anyone into his confidence until that person has won his full trust and respect. The Dog is not given to quick romances or short-lived relationships but likes his friendships to evolve over a longer period of time. Similarly many a Dog has had a long courtship before he decides to marry. Unfortunately, in spite of his many admirable qualities, matters of the heart do not always run smoothly for the Dog. He can be sensitive and keenly aware of the feelings of others and, if the source of his love should give him any sign of a waning of affection or cause for jealousy, the Dog can become anxious and insecure and this can undermine many a relationship.

The Dog is also not the easiest person to live with. He can be an anxious person, worry a great deal and be cynical and pessimistic in outlook. He can be forthright and stubborn but, against this, he is intensely loyal and supportive and will love, honour and protect his partner dearly. He tries to establish a secure and stable home life – the Dog attaches much importance to his home and makes sure it is well and comfortably furnished. He also has a tendency towards nostalgia and 'the good old times' and his home is likely to contain many mementoes of his earlier years as well as family heirlooms and antiques.

The Dog makes a fine and dutiful parent. He devotes much time and attention to his children although, in view of his anxious nature, he can be prone to worry unduly over them, and especially about their progress and behaviour.

The female Dog tends to be more sociable and outgoing than the male. She also has a broader range of interests as well as having a wider circle of friends. She has a charming and friendly manner, converses well and is a good judge of character. As with all Dogs, she is caring and attentive and willingly helps and supports those in need. She sets about her activities in a responsible and diligent way and is greatly loved by her family and friends. She is often attractive in her looks and usually chooses simple but practical clothes.

The male Dog can be most distinguished in his appearance and often has an impeccable taste in clothes. He likes to keep himself active and in trim and, for recreation, may enjoy taking part in sport and outdoor activities.

The Dog has a sociable nature and enjoys the company of others. However, he much prefers small social gatherings to large parties or lavish functions. He does not like pretension and prefers the opportunity to talk to and listen to others rather than engage in small talk or mix with lots of strangers. At bigger functions the Dog can easily become introverted and morose but when he is in company he likes he will truly shine. He can be a witty speaker, a marvellous raconteur as well as being an attentive and considerate listener.

The Dog has a practical nature and enjoys carrying out DIY projects in his home and garden. He also plans his activities with care – he is not one who likes or adapts well to change. He is not materialistic in his outlook and while he may enjoy spending money when he has it – Dogs can be spendthrifts – he is not preoccupied with the pursuit of wealth.

The Dog has many fine qualities and throughout his life will win the admiration of many. Those who meet him appreciate his honesty, dependability and his caring and selfless nature. He has a good heart and is well meaning. His main weakness, however, is his tendency to worry. Some of the time these worries are unfounded and of his own making and if the Dog were to confide more willingly in others or look more optimistically on matters, he would find his life much easier.

This tendency to worry may affect the Dog throughout his life and lead to periods of uncertainty. As a child the Dog is affectionate and loving and will strive to please his parents and teachers. He is diligent, alert and well behaved. However, in his formative years, the Dog child needs much love, support and encouragement – if it is not given his confidence and self-esteem may be greatly undermined.

His youth can prove a challenging time. While he will impress others with his responsible and diligent manner, matters of the heart may not always go smoothly. Although he has a romantic and passionate nature and desires to establish a secure, close and loving relationship, he is acutely aware of the feelings of others and this can cause him much anguish.

As he matures the Dog may become more settled and provided he feels inspired in his work, he can enjoy considerable success. However, despite this, the Dog may still be prone to bouts of uncertainty and pessimism and he would be helped if he were to confide more readily in others rather than keep his worries to himself. As old age approaches, the Dog may rue the opportunities he has missed or things he has not done, but he can take heart. Although there may have been periods of difficulty and of disappointment, there will also have been times of splendid achievements and of things accomplished. He should think, too, of all the good he has done, the friends and causes he has supported and of the many who hold him in such high esteem.

The French writer Voltaire was a Dog and he once wrote, 'Whatever you do, stamp out abuses, and love those who love you.' Throughout the Dog's rich and fulfilling life he will indeed stand up for what he believes is right as well as loving his family and friends dearly.

Famous Dogs

Andre Agassi, Jane Asher, Brigitte Bardot, Candice Bergman, David Bowie, Kate Bush, José Carreras, Cher, Sir Winston Churchill, Bill Clinton, Jamie Lee Curtis, Charles Dance, Christopher Dean, Sally Field, Judy Garland, Lenny Henry, Barry Humphries, Michael Jackson, Felicity Kendal, Maureen Lipman, Sophia Loren, Joanna Lumley, Shirley MacLaine, Patrick MacNee, Madonna, Norman Mailer, Barry Manilow, Rik Mayall, Liza Minelli, David Niven, Elvis Presley, Linda Ronstadt, Sade, Jennifer Saunders, Norman Schwarzkopf, Sylvester Stallone, Donald Sutherland, Chris Tarrant, Mother Teresa, Ben Vereen, Prince William, Shelley Winters.

THE PIG

Key characteristics: Sincere, honest, trusting, genial, sociable, reliable, hard working, well meaning, but naïve and stubborn.

In love: Passionate, sensual and loyal.

Although in the West it is not flattering to call someone a pig, those born under the twelfth and final Chinese sign have many fine virtues – so much so that, in Chinese horoscopes, being a Pig is both a compliment and honour.

Pigs are born under the sign of honesty. The Pig is sincere, trusting and relates well to others. He has a genial and often jovial nature and people feel at ease in his company. He enjoys socializing and has a fondness for the good things in life. He likes wining and dining and is often a keen partygoer. The Pig is a pleasure seeker.

The Pig also has a wide range of interests, although more often than not he prefers to dip into subjects rather than become a specialist. He is a keen reader and may also like gardening and the countryside. The Pig, with his sincere interest in others, can often become involved in charitable causes or do much to help those less fortunate than himself. He is generous, well meaning and has a deep faith in the goodness of mankind. Unfortunately, however, this faith is sometimes abused and there are some who take advantage of the Pig's good nature. The Pig can be both gullible and naive but even though some may let him down, he is not vindictive and does not harbour a grudge. Nor does he like to be involved in confrontational situations – he is a peacemaker, will do his utmost to steer clear of arguments and disputes and will strive to remain on good terms with all around him.

Although the Pig may not be as competitive as some signs, he is diligent and persevering and his loyalty and integrity is much appreciated by his employers. However, it sometimes takes him a little while – and several false starts – before he decides what he really wants to do and finds where his talents really lie. He learns well from experience and has a resilient and usually optimistic nature. He is also patient and if there is a position he wants or has an objective to reach he will strive long and hard until he has achieved his goal. The Pig has a wide range of talents and he often does well in commerce, the medical profession, law, teaching and, with his practical nature, in craftwork. Many Pigs are also attracted to careers in show business or in some aspect of the arts.

The Pig has considerable earning ability and is usually blessed with good fortune in money matters. This is just as well for the Pig enjoys money and the comforts it can buy. He can be self-indulgent and also most generous – the Pig takes great delight in buying presents for others – but while he may enjoy spending money, he still keeps a close watch on his expenditure and can be a shrewd investor.

The Pig attaches great importance to his social life and particularly enjoys small social gatherings. He likes the opportunity for meeting and mixing with others and, with his friendly and easygoing manner, he gets on well with most people. He is a good and attentive listener as well as being a lively speaker. The Pig does, however, tend to have a fondness for earthy humour and sometimes lacks refinement. He enjoys dressing up and both male and female Pigs can be fashionable and stylish dressers.

The Pig values his relations with others and in matters of the heart is sensuous and passionate. In his youth he can be promiscuous and flirtatious and throws himself fully into his relationships – so much so, that if things do go wrong he can suffer much emotional anguish and bitter disappointment. However, the Pig chooses his partner with care and once he settles down he will be loyal and faithful and makes a fine and caring spouse.

The Pig's family and home life is most important to him and he strives to give his home a calm and harmonious atmosphere. The Pig tends to have a great interest in the culinary arts and takes much pleasure in preparing lavish meals, catering and in hosting parties.

The Pig makes a loving and protective parent. He makes sure his children want for nothing but at the same time is a keen educationalist and guides them well in their various activities. Children relate well to the Pig parent although, being so protective, he may have problems dealing with some of the more independent-minded signs.

The female Pig has a particularly lively and engaging manner. She is sociable, sincere and trusting. She is attentive to her partner and her children and devotes herself unselfishly to their needs. She also has many interests – especially craftwork, gardening and reading – but it is her family and home that are her real joy in life. The female Pig is not as career orientated as some other signs.

The male Pig has an agreeable and amiable manner and is well liked, but underneath his genial nature, the male Pig also possesses a stubborn streak and can be quite obstinate at times.

As regards the Pig's weaknesses, he can be indulgent and greedy as well as being gullible. He can be hesitant in his actions and not always willing to take the initiative. However, when he has no alternative or has some objective he wishes to obtain, he will act with fortitude and vigour. Also, in his desire to please, the Pig sometimes over-commits himself and takes on more activities than he can sensibly handle. There are occasions when it would be in everyone's interests for the Pig to be a little more discerning. However, the Pig is well intentioned and his integrity, friendliness and genial manner is greatly admired and valued by others.

The Pig invariably leads an active life, and his childhood is often an exceptionally happy time. The Pig child has an affectionate nature, is generally well behaved and popular. Even in his formative years, though, the Pig's pleasure-seeking ways are evident, and he may need firm guidance if he is not to fall behind in his schoolwork. For the Pig child, his friends, and interests – especially if they involve the great outdoors – are his priority.

The Pig makes the most of his youth. He leads an active social life and has many romantic attachments – some of which will bring him much pleasure, some disappointment. However, once he settles down he will be keenly aware of his new responsibilities and will be loyal and attentive to his partner.

As the Pig matures he strives to do well in his career. Although he lacks competitive spirit he is patient, resilient and hard working and his talents will be recognized, encouraged and valued by others. Often, after a slow and sometimes bumpy start, the Pig enjoys much success in his chosen line of work. In addition to the successes and material comforts that his work will bring, the Pig takes much delight in the activities of his family and his social life. The Pig's old age is often a time of contentment, when he will enjoy the fruits of his labours and the comforts he has acquired.

The American poet and essayist Ralph Waldo Emerson was born under the sign of the Pig and his words are true for many who share this sign:

> To laugh often and much; to win the respect of intelligent people and the affection of children; to earn the appreciation of honest critics and endure the betrayal of false friends; to appreciate beauty; to find the best in others; to leave the world a bit better whether by a healthy child, a garden patch, or a redeemed social condition; to know even one life has breathed easier because you lived. This is to have succeeded.

In life, many Pigs deservedly succeed.

Famous Pigs

Bryan Adams, Woody Allen, Julie Andrews, Fred Astaire, Sir Richard Attenborough, Lucille Ball, Bobby Davro, Humphrey Bogart, Richard Chamberlain, Hillary Clinton, Glenn Close, Noel Coward, the Dalai Lama, Sheena Easton, Emmylou Harris, Ernest Hemingway, Henry VIII, King Hussein of Jordan, Elton John, Carl Gustav Jung, Nastassja Kinski, Kevin Kline, Hugh Laurie, Jerry Lee Lewis, Johnny Mathis, Dudley Moore, Wolfgang Amadeus Mozart, Marie Osmond, Luciano Pavarotti, Prince Rainier of Monaco, Ronald Reagan, Lee Remick, Ginger Rogers, Pete Sampras, Arnold Schwarzenegger, Steven Spielberg, Emma Thompson, Topol, Michael Winner, Tracey Ullman, the Duchess of York.

Part Two

RELATIONS BETWEEN THE SIGNS

Rat and Rat

General Relations

The Rat delights in the company of others and when it is another lively and sociable Rat, the two can have much fun together. Between them they have many interests they can share and, as both enjoy conversation, they may while away many a happy hour locked in intense discussion. There is often a good understanding and rapport between them.

When two Rats work together their combined skills can bring them considerable success. Both are enterprising, both opportunist and both keen to make the most of their many skills. They are resourceful, with drive and ambition. When two Rats work purposefully towards a specific goal they make a formidable team. However, a certain discipline is necessary if they are to make the most of their talents. Rats sometimes spread their energies too widely and become involved in more activities than they can sensibly handle. If they can control their sometimes restless and greedy natures, then a working relationship between them goes well.

In the parent–child relationship there is a great bond between the Rat parent and Rat child. They understand each other well and the Rat parent takes much delight in encouraging and guiding his enterprising child. The Rat child thrives in the loving and protective atmosphere of a close-knit Rat home and is a source of much pride to his parents. The Rat parent and child love and support each other dearly and theirs is a close and valuable relationship.

In Love and Marriage

The attraction between two Rats is strong. Both are romantic and passionate and they have a good understanding of each other. They are outgoing and sociable and together have a wide range of interests. Both delight in socializing, entertaining and travelling and may have a fondness for literature and the arts.

They are also likely to share similar outlooks. Both value their security and are keen to make the most of their abilities. They support and encourage each other well and remain mindful of each other's advice.

They place much value on their home life and, if they have children, make caring and protective parents. Rats value their family bonds and the Rat family is likely to be closely knit. Although Rats can be indulgent, a Rat couple handles financial matters well; most are financially secure and able to enjoy a comfortable standard of living.

A Rat couple can find much happiness together but they would do well to maintain some separate interests rather than insist on complete togetherness in everything they do. Also, if they face problems, Rats can be frank, forthright and highly critical and this may sometimes lead to acrimonious exchanges between them.

However, as a couple they strive to overcome any problems that may arise – Rats are both resourceful and resilient – and they make a close, loving and devoted pair. There is a strong empathy between two Rats and in love and marriage they are well suited.

RAT AND OX

General Relations

Although the Rat and Ox have very different personalities – the Rat being far more outgoing than the Ox – these two signs get on well together. They trust and respect each other and can become firm friends. The Rat may prefer a more active social life to the Ox, but they do have interests they can share and each enjoys the company of the other. The Rat particularly appreciates the Ox's confident and steadfast nature, while the Ox delights in the vivacity and charm of the Rat. General relations between the Rat and Ox are often excellent.

The Rat and Ox also work well together and, as colleagues or business partners, can achieve considerable success. Both are ambitious and work hard and their different skills are highly complementary. The Rat is a past master at PR and customer relations while the Ox provides method, order and consistency. They recognize and capitalize on each other's strengths and there is a great deal of trust and respect between them. Together they can build up an excellent working relationship.

In the parent–child relationship there is again a strong bond. The Rat parent admires the industry and conscientiousness of the Ox child and not only does much to encourage the Ox child but helps the child to become more outgoing and less reserved. When the Ox is parent and Rat the child, the Ox parent delights in the versatility of the Rat child but provides enough discipline and guidance for the Rat child to use his talents and energies wisely. There is much love and respect between them. In both cases the children will thrive in the loving, secure and protective atmosphere of a Rat or Ox home.

In Love and Marriage

There is a strong attraction between the Rat and Ox and, in love and marriage, they can find much happiness. The character differences that exist between them often prove complementary and each loves , values and admires the other dearly.

The Rat is the more outgoing of the two and the Ox gains from the Rat's vivacity, love of life and sociable nature. Under the Rat's influence the Ox may become more outgoing and more at ease in his relations with others. The Ox also admires the resourcefulness and enterprise of the Rat and finds the Rat invigorating company. Similarly, the Rat admires the Ox's loyalty, strength of character and ambition. The Rat feels reassured by having such a resolute and reliable partner. Although the Ox may not be so keen a socializer as the Rat, they do have interests they can share. Both attach much importance to their home life and take equal delight in creating and maintaining their home and, if they have children, they make caring and conscientious parents.

The Rat and Ox also seek stability and security in their lives and with the Rat's thrift and Ox's careful nature, most Rat and Ox couples are materially well off and able to enjoy a good standard of living.

In their relationship each is mindful of the other. The Ox is a steadying influence over the sometimes over-active Rat, while the Rat adds colour and variety to the Ox's cautious and conservative nature. In their different ways the Rat and Ox complement each other superbly well.

In love and marriage the Rat and Ox are ideally suited and this can be a happy, satisfying and beneficial relationship for both signs. An often excellent match.

RAT AND TIGER

General Relations

The Rat and Tiger are two lively and outgoing signs and they generally get on well together. Both are keen socializers and, with their wide interests, they invariably have activities they can share. The Tiger is very much taken with the Rat's charm and personable manner while the Rat enjoys the Tiger's vibrant, enthusiastic and confident personality. There is a good understanding between them.

When the Rat and Tiger work together each is quick to appreciate the strengths of the other. The Rat values the Tiger's enterprise and enthusiasm, while the Tiger recognizes the Rat's resourcefulness and ability to spot opportunities. Both are ambitious and both are capable of devising many wonderful and innovative ideas. There is considerable respect between them and when they are committed to a specific objective, their combined enthusiasm, drive and resourcefulness helps guide them to success.

In the parent–child relationship the Rat parent may be proud of the versatility and enterprise of his Tiger child but the child's independent-mindedness leads to clashes. The Rat is a protective parent and the Tiger child is not one for staying in the fold. When the Tiger is parent and Rat the child, the Tiger parent encourages the Rat in his wide range of interests and enjoys the Rat child's spirited nature. However, the Rat child values a secure and stable environment and may sometimes feel ill at ease with the restlessness of a Tiger parent.

In Love and Marriage

The Rat and Tiger are often attracted to each other. Both have lively and sociable natures and they enjoy each other's company.

They are also both highly passionate signs and the physical attraction between them is strong.

The Rat and Tiger have many interests they can share. Both like socializing and going out and both may also be keen travellers. They have adventurous and outgoing natures and relate well to each other. The Tiger delights in the Rat's charming and sociable manner as well as appreciating the Rat's skills as a homemaker. The Rat in turn finds reassurance in the Tiger's confident and ebullient manner. They support each other well and there is much love between them.

However, while the Rat and Tiger can find happiness together, there are some problems that they need to address. Their different attitudes to money may cause problems. The Tiger tends to be generous in his spending while the Rat is more thrifty, and this may lead to friction between them. In addition the Rat may feel unsettled by the Tiger's restless nature and the Rat needs to accept that the Tiger desires a certain amount of independence and allow him time to pursue his own individual interests. Both can be frank and forthright in expressing their views and this may give rise to some heated exchanges.

With two such lively and forceful personalities problems will arise in their relationship, but the Rat and Tiger mean much to each other and, with goodwill and understanding on both sides, they should be able to reconcile their differences.

In love and marriage their relationship may not always be harmonious, but they do have interests they can share, they understand each other well and there is much love and passion between them. With care, this can be a reasonably good match.

RAT AND RABBIT

General Relations

Although the Rat and Rabbit are both sociable signs and possess considerable charm, neither cares much for the other. The Rabbit, who has a calm and tranquil manner, feels ill at ease with the active and energetic Rat, while the Rat considers the Rabbit reserved and over-sensitive. They may delight in a once in a while conversation but rarely become close friends.

When the Rat and Rabbit work together, however, their different skills may prove complementary. The Rabbit appreciates the Rat's skills at seeking out opportunities as well as his more outgoing and action-oriented nature, while the Rat values the Rabbit's organizational talents, shrewd judgement and commercial acumen. If they can unite in pursuing a specific objective they may make an effective and successful combination. However, due to their different personalities, neither may feel completely at ease when working with the other.

In the parent–child relationship relations between these two signs need to be handled with considerable care. When the Rat is parent and Rabbit the child, the Rabbit child may be sensitive to the Rat parent's frank and forthright nature as well as feeling uneasy with all the activity and bustle found in a Rat household. The Rabbit child prefers a calmer and more settled environment and unless care is taken there may be a certain distance between parent and child. When the Rabbit is parent and Rat the child, the Rabbit parent may admire the versatility of the Rat child but find the child's lively and boisterous nature a disruptive influence on his calm and orderly existence.

In Love and Marriage

The Rat and Rabbit are two passionate and sensual signs and

there may be a strong physical attraction between them. Both are charming and sociable and they have many interests in common. They are both homelovers, are keen socializers and may share an interest in literature and the arts. The early stages of their relationship may bring much happiness, but the longer they know each other, the more difficult their relationship may become. Their temperaments are ill suited and, in love and marriage, a match between them may prove difficult and challenging.

The Rat is an active and energetic sign and tends to involve himself in a multitude of activities and interests. The Rabbit, however, seeks a much quieter and more settled lifestyle and feels anxious at the constant activity of the Rat. Also the Rat tends to be forthright and sometimes critical in his manner and this, too, can disturb the more sensitive Rabbit. The Rat may find the cautious nature of the Rabbit a restrictive influence while the Rabbit may find the Rat brash and overbearing.

If the Rat and Rabbit can adjust and adapt to each other then a relationship between them may survive. Together they could devote time to their joint interests as well as pour much energy into their beloved home. Each may also learn from the other, the Rat becoming more refined and better organized and the Rabbit becoming more outgoing. However, it takes a major effort on both their parts to make the adjustments necessary and a match between them may – despite their fine individual qualities – be difficult.

RAT AND DRAGON

General Relations

The Rat and Dragon get on extremely well together. They are both lively, outgoing and sociable signs and they enjoy each other's company. They have many interests in common and there is a great deal of trust and understanding between them. The Rat and Dragon may often become close and lifelong friends.

Their respect and liking for each other also translates itself to a working situation and when the Rat and Dragon work together they can enjoy considerable success. Both are ambitious, enterprising and work hard, and each values the skills of the other. The Dragon, in particular, appreciates the Rat's ability to seek out opportunities and his skills at PR, while the Rat values the Dragon's resolute and confident manner. They trust and support each other and in business make a formidable and successful team.

In the parent–child relationship relations between these two signs are again good. The lively and amiable Rat child responds well to his Dragon parent and there is a close bond between them. When the Rat is parent and Dragon the child, the Dragon child learns much from the Rat parent and the parent provides all the love, encouragement and discipline that the Dragon child needs. In both cases there is much love between the parents and children of these signs and the parent has good reason to be proud of his enterprising and resourceful Rat or Dragon child.

In Love and Marriage

This is a splendid match and in love and marriage the Rat and Dragon can find much happiness. They are ideally suited and their personalities complement each other well.

The Rat greatly admires the confident, determined and honourable nature of the Dragon and finds the Dragon lively and enjoyable company. Similarly, the Dragon loves the charm and sociable nature of the Rat as well as appreciating the Rat's resourcefulness and versatility. They support and encourage each other and there is considerable empathy between them.

The Dragon also delights in the Rat's caring and attentive ways – the Rat is one of the few signs who knows how to get round the Dragon! They love each other dearly and, as both have passionate and sensual natures, the physical attraction between them is strong – together the Rat and Dragon have much fun.

They also have many interests they can share; both are keen socializers and take much pleasure in entertaining and travel. They value their home life and, if they have children, make caring and attentive parents.

The Rat and Dragon benefit from each other's strengths. The Rat is a steadying influence on the sometimes impulsive nature of the Dragon, while the Rat feels reassured by having such a confident partner. In their relationship each is mindful of the views and advice of the other.

The relationship between the Rat and Dragon is one of the best for both signs and together they find much happiness and contentment. An excellent match.

RAT AND SNAKE

General Relations

The Rat and Snake like and respect each other and general relations between them are often good. The Rat has many interests, a lively repartee and a charm that the Snake finds irresistible. The Rat in turn admires the Snake's calm, collected and thoughtful nature. They enjoy each other's company and, while their tastes may not always converge – the Rat is much more a partygoer and socializer than the Snake – these two signs always have time for each other.

In business matters the Rat and Snake work well together and as colleagues and business partners they may enjoy considerable success. Each recognizes the other's strengths and in many ways they complement each other. The Snake is the planner, organizer and adviser while the more action-orientated Rat sets the plans into motion. The Snake also happily leaves the persuasive Rat to win over their customers but at the same time is a useful curb on some of the Rat's more risky notions. Both are ambitious, opportunist and materialistic and together they make a formidable combination.

In a parent–child relationship relations between these two signs are again good. The Rat child responds well to the quiet, caring and loving ways of a Snake parent. The Snake parent encourages the Rat child's multitude of interests and there is a good rapport between them. Their sense of fun also helps unite them. When the Rat is parent and Snake the child, the Rat parent relates well to the Snake child and helps draw the often quiet and withdrawn child out of his shell. The Snake child gains much from having a firm, but loving, Rat parent.

In Love and Marriage

The attraction between these two signs is strong. The Rat is captivated by the Snake's quiet and seductive charm, while the Snake is drawn to the Rat's warm, friendly and sensual nature. There is a powerful sexual chemistry between these two signs and in love and marriage they can form a loving, happy and generally harmonious relationship.

The Rat and Snake often have similar outlooks. Both are opportunists and both go through life intent on making the best of their abilities and skills. Both are resourceful and in their relationship the Rat and Snake do much to help, support and encourage the other. They also gain from their different strengths. The Rat benefits from the Snake's planning, organization and wise counsel, while the Snake values the resourcefulness and determined spirit of the Rat. Both enjoy the material comforts in life and each aims for a high level of security.

The Rat and Snake also share many interests. Both are imaginative, enjoy intelligent discussion and may share a fondness for literature and the arts. They make caring and attentive parents and happily devote much time and energy to the upbringing of any children they have.

Relations between the Rat and Snake are invariably good, although there are certain elements in their personalities that may cause problems. The Snake prefers to conduct his activities in a calm and measured way and may not always appreciate the Rat's more aggressive and blustering style. Similarly, the Rat may feel restricted by the Snake's possessive nature. The Rat likes a certain freedom of action and may find the Snake's attitude something of a restraint. If, as is likely, both signs recognize these possible problem areas and try to adapt to each other, then their relationship is likely to be secure and enduring. In love and marriage the Rat and Snake have much to offer each other and can find happiness and contentment. A good match.

RAT AND HORSE

General Relations

The Rat and Horse are both outgoing signs and for a short time may find each other interesting company. They are both keen socializers and have interests they can share. However, their different temperaments may bring them into conflict and it is rare for the Rat and Horse to become lasting friends. Both signs can be strong willed, opinionated and forthright in their views and this may lead to clashes between them. There is not much empathy between them and general relations between these two signs are often poor.

Problems also emerge when the Rat and Horse work together,

either as colleagues or business partners. Both may be oppor-tunists and possess good business skills, but each wants to take the lead and dominate. There is mistrust between them; the Horse comes to view the Rat as conniving and thrifty, while the Rat sees the Horse as impulsive, impatient and short tempered. There is little agreement between them and their competitive and independent spirits get the better of them – not a happy or successful arrangement.

In the parent–child relationship relations between these two signs may again be fraught with difficulties. The Rat makes a protective and loving parent but may have difficulty in coping with the restless and independent nature of a Horse child. The Horse child craves for independence, freedom and liberty while the Rat strives for a close-knit family. When the Horse is parent and Rat the child, the Rat child may feel unnerved by the activity and volatility that exists in a Horse household. The Rat child seeks security and stability and as a consequence relations between Horse parent and Rat child may prove awkward.

In Love and Marriage

Both the Rat and Horse are romantic and passionate and they may fall deeply in love with each other. The Horse is seduced by the Rat's irresistible charm and the Rat by the Horse's lively and engaging manner. In the early stages of their relationship they have much fun and each delights in the affection, wit and wisdom of the other. The early days are passionate and blissful.

However, the long-term prospects for such a match are bleak. Generally, once the Rat and Horse have overcome the initial enthusiasm of their meeting, relations between them quickly degenerate. Both the Rat and Horse are strong-willed and opin-ionated signs. Both are egoists and both want to dominate the relationship. The Rat is open and forthright in expressing his views and has little trouble in igniting the Horse's short temper. There is likely to be much dissension between them.

The Rat also finds it hard to come to terms with the Horse's restless and independent attitude, while the Horse finds the Rat meddlesome and too much of a restrictive influence. Nor does the Horse want to spend as much time at home as the home-loving Rat. Their differing attitudes towards money may also cause problems. The thrifty Rat likes to keep a close control over the purse strings and views the Horse as a spendthrift and over-generous, while the Horse considers the Rat materialistic and tight fisted.

The Chinese do not recommend a match between these two signs and after the initial flames of passion have cooled, this may prove a turbulent and stormy relationship. In love and marriage this is a difficult match.

RAT AND GOAT

General Relations

Both the Rat and Goat know how to enjoy themselves and have a fondness for the good life. Together they enjoy wining, dining and leading an active social life. Both signs have considerable charm and enjoy each other's company. For the short to medium term the Rat and Goat can become good friends but each has traits which irritate the other and in time they may drift apart. With the Rat and Goat it is a case of enjoying their friendship while it lasts.

The Rat and Goat do not work well together and when they are colleagues or business partners difficulties are almost certain to emerge. The Rat is a supreme opportunist, constantly geared up for action and determined to make the most of his abilities. He is competitive and ambitious. The Goat, however, does not possess the drive of the Rat. To do well, the Goat needs to feel inspired and encouraged by others. The Rat is a self-starter, the Goat needs to be prodded. The Rat views the Goat's hesitant attitude with misgivings, while the Goat feels ill at ease with the Rat's aggressive and thrifty attitude. In work they are best going their separate ways.

In the parent–child relationship the Goat child values the love and security found in a Rat home. The Rat likes to maintain a close-knit family and this suits the Goat child. When the Goat is the parent and Rat the child, the Rat child appreciates the love and affection of the Goat parent, but may feel uneasy with the Goat's capriciousness and lack of routine. Similarly, the Rat child's adventurous nature may sometimes concern the Goat. The Goat parent strives for a quiet and peaceful existence, but this may not always be possible with a boisterous Rat child about.

In Love and Marriage

The Rat and Goat are both friendly and sociable signs and are often attracted to each other. Both possess romantic and passionate natures and both exude a strong sex appeal. Relations between them in the early stages of their courtship are excellent. They share many interests, like to lead an active social life and can have much fun together.

However, such a blissful relationship is hard to maintain and the longer-term prospects for a match between the Rat and Goat are decidedly bleak. As the intensity of their feelings begins to fade they begin to discover the gulf that exists between them.

The Rat is hardworking, industrious and energetic, while the Goat sets about his activities in a much more leisurely manner. Nor does the Goat share the ambitious nature of the Rat. The Rat is thrifty while the Goat is a spendthrift. The Rat can be forthright and candid in his views, while the Goat is sensitive, shrinks from arguments and takes the Rat's criticisms very much to heart. The Rat also has little time for the Goat's artistic and sometimes whimsical nature and loses patience with the Goat's ca-priciousness. The Goat, however, may come to view the Rat as greedy, meddlesome and fussy. From a relationship which started out with such promise, both sides may prove to be disap-pointed.

However, if both are prepared to make the effort and devote themselves to their joint interests – particularly as both are so home and family orientated – then it is just possible they may make their relationship work. But generally, because of their different outlooks and attitudes, this is often a difficult and chal-lenging match.

Rat and Monkey

General Relations

With their lively and sociable natures the Rat and Monkey get on well together. Each greatly admires the other and with their many mutual interests and their great sense of fun they relate well to each other. The Rat delights in the Monkey's resourceful-ness, wit and keen intellect while the Monkey enjoys the Rat's charm, drive and ambition. Together they may pass many a happy hour in each other's company and may become close and lasting friends.

Their rapport also serves them well when they work together. In many ways they are two of a kind. Both are cunning, oppor-tunist and determined to succeed. Both recognize the drive and commitment in the other and together they make a strong team. Each inspires and motivates the other. The main danger, though, is if either – and particularly the Monkey – tries to go one better than the other. Each is crafty and each may be tempted to outwit the other. However, such a tactic would be ill advised as both are masters in the art of self-preservation. If they can both keep their attention firmly on their joint objectives then, with their combined resourcefulness and ingenuity, they could enjoy considerable success.

In the parent–child relationship the Rat parent admires the resourcefulness, humour and versatility of a Monkey child and the child responds well to the Rat's firm but kindly guidance. There is a close bond between them. When the Monkey is parent and Rat the child, the Rat child is very fond of his Monkey parent and strives to live up to the Monkey's expectations. The Monkey parent does much to encourage the Rat child in his wide range of interests. In both cases, the parents and children of these signs have imaginative and resourceful natures and understand each other well.

In Love and Marriage

The attraction between a Rat and Monkey is strong and in love and marriage they can find much happiness. With their many mutual interests and similar outlooks they are well matched and make a close and loving couple.

Both the Rat and Monkey have sociable and outgoing natures and like to live life to the full. They are action-oriented signs and keep themselves well occupied with their many interests. Both are keen socializers and between them have many friends. They take great pleasure in entertaining at home but are equally content wining and dining in the best places in town. Rats and Monkeys like to live well and, with their money-making talents, most Rat–Monkey couples are financially secure.

They are also both immensely resourceful. They are ambitious, opportunist and determined to make the most of their abilities. They support and encourage each other well and both value the strengths and skills of the other. The Monkey, in particular, appreciates the Rat for his loyalty, judgement, enthusiasm and skills as a homemaker. The Rat tends to be more disciplined and persistent than the Monkey and this, too, could be in the Monkey's interests. The Rat, in turn, delights in the Monkey's lively nature, quick wit, resourcefulness and enterprise. Between them they further their joint interests and while the Rat is more home orientated than the Monkey, together they devote much time and energy to their home and to any children they have. Also, as both have a good sense of humour, there is a strong element of fun in their relationship.

As a couple they are ideally suited, and love and respect each other dearly. In love and marriage the Rat and Monkey make an excellent match.

Rat and Rooster

General Relations

Although the Rat and Rooster are two sociable and outgoing signs they do not relate well to each other. The Rat dislikes the vanity and egoism of the Rooster, while the Rooster finds the Rat too opportunist and manipulative. Neither places much trust in the other. Although both may enjoy conversation, they can be notoriously blunt in their views and their outspokenness may prove the death-knell for any friendship that might have existed between them. General relations between the Rat and Rooster are often poor.

The Rat and Rooster also do not work well together, either as colleagues or business partners. Although both are hard workers, the Rooster plans his activities to the finest detail and is highly organized, while the Rat is supreme at taking advantage of a situation and places great reliance on his charm and resourcefulness. The Rat finds the Rooster too much of a restraining and inhibiting influence, while the Rooster dislikes the opportunistic ways of the Rat. There are also conflicts over finance. The Rooster tends to be a spendthrift, while the Rat is thrifty. There is little understanding or agreement between them and their working relationship is fraught with difficulties – not a successful combination.

In the parent–child relationship the Rat child values the security and sense of order that exists in a Rooster home. However, the Rat child is one who needs much love and support and may sometimes feel unsettled by the strict and forthright tones of a Rooster parent. There may be a certain edginess to their relationship but the resourceful Rat child is still a source of much pride to the Rooster parent. When the Rat is parent and Rooster the child, the Rooster child delights in the vivacity and affection of a Rat parent but dislikes the lack of order and routine that is so often missing in a Rat household. The Rat parent may also have problems dealing with the strong and independent-minded ways of a Rooster child. In both cases relations between parent and child need careful handling.

In Love and Marriage

The Rat and Rooster are both lively and outgoing signs and initially there may be a strong attraction between them. The Rooster may be attracted by the Rat's charm and personable nature, while the Rat admires the confident and ebullient ways of the Rooster. Both like to lead an active social life, are keen partygoers and both have a deep love of conversation. In the early stages of their relationship they may have much fun together, each charmed by the qualities of the other. However, the longer-term prospects are difficult and each sign needs to make major adjustments if they are to remain together. In love and marriage this can be a challenging match.

Although they may share similar interests, their different personality traits may bring them into conflict. Both are forceful characters, both with a mind of their own and each tries to dominate the relationship.

The Rooster is precise, orderly and well organized and likes to follow a set routine, while the Rat prefers to live from day to day making the best of every opportunity that comes along. The Rooster considers the Rat unmethodical, while the Rat finds the Rooster inflexible in his outlook. Neither shows much willingness to change his ways and conflicts and disagreements are sure to follow. In their relationship there is likely to be much arguing and bickering and, with their forthright natures, each may be critical of the other.

Problems can also emerge over finance. The Rat is thrifty, while the Rooster tends to be a spendthrift and, to the Rat's mind, over-generous. The Rat also likes to keep close tabs on all around him and the Rooster could resent this.

Both the Rat and Rooster are strong minded and strong willed and their relationship may be fraught with difficulties. If they can concentrate on their joint interests and accept each other for what they are, then their relationship may just work. But it will not be easy and after the initial flames of romance have died away, their relationship could be difficult and turbulent.

RAT AND DOG

General Relations

The Rat and Dog enjoy each other's company and may become reasonably good friends. The Rat admires the loyal and trusting nature of the Dog, while the Dog enjoys the sociable and outgoing ways of the Rat. Together they may pass many a happy hour socializing and exchanging views. Admittedly they may not agree on everything, but they do respect each other.

When the Rat and Dog work together they may not always be in full agreement but they may still benefit from each other's individual strengths. The Dog is not as materialistic as the Rat and the Dog may feel uneasy with the Rat's opportunistic and sometimes manipulative ways. Similarly the thrifty Rat may despair of the Dog's spendthrift tendency or not fully appreciate his idealistic views. However, if they can reconcile their differences, the Dog can gain from the Rat's confident and enterprising nature, while the Dog will bring order, method and discipline to the Rat's ways of working. With care they can establish a satisfactory working relationship.

In the parent–child relationship the Dog child values the love and encouragement of a Rat parent, although he may sometimes feel uncomfortable with the Rat parent's restlessness. The Dog child likes order and routine and this is something not always found in an active and bustling Rat household. When the Dog is parent and Rat the child, the Rat child delights the Dog parent with his wide-ranging abilities and genial nature. The Rat child also greatly values the secure and protective atmosphere of a Dog home. In both cases, and despite any differences that may exist between them, there is always a close and enduring bond between them.

In Love and Marriage

The Rat and Dog both possess qualities that the other admires and in love and marriage they can form a satisfactory relationship. Each can benefit from the other although there are areas that may cause problems and that they need to address if they are to live in harmony.

The Rat greatly admires the loyalty and dependability of the Dog. The Rat trusts the Dog implicitly and the Dog is a steadying influence on the Rat's sometimes over-exuberant ways. The Rat is mindful of the Dog's advice and the Dog is a useful curb on the Rat's impulsive nature and brings more order and method into the Rat's lifestyle. The Dog, in turn, delights in the Rat's charming, sociable and loving nature. The resourceful Rat instils confidence in the Dog and does much to alleviate some of his worries and anxieties.

Both the Rat and Dog value their relationship. They are both romantic and passionate signs and attach much importance to their home. They each strive to make their home comfortable and 'homely' and, with their strong family ties, it is likely to be full of family heirlooms, mementoes of childhood and other items of nostalgia.

However, while the Rat and Dog can find happiness together, problems may still arise between them. The Rat is thrifty and careful with his money, while the Dog is, in the Rat's eyes, over-generous and a spendthrift. Similarly the Rat can be restless and enjoys change and challenges, while the Dog appreciates consistency and careful planning and does not adapt so well to change.

If they can reconcile their differences then the Rat and Dog can enjoy a content and fulfilling relationship. In love and marriage they can each learn and benefit from the other and often make a good and lasting match.

RAT AND PIG

General Relations

The Rat and Pig have many interests in common and often become close and loyal friends. They are both outgoing, like socializing and have a fondness for the good things in life. They enjoy each other's company and often share similar viewpoints. There is a good rapport and understanding between them and general relations between these two signs are often excellent.

The Rat and Pig also work well together and, as colleagues or business partners, they can enjoy much success. Both work hard and diligently and both have entrepreneurial flair. The Pig delights in the Rat's skill in seeking out opportunities and developing ideas, while the Rat appreciates the Pig's commercial acumen and ability to make money. They are enterprising and ambitious as well as being determined to make the most of their considerable abilities. Providing the Rat does not try to take advantage of the Pig's trusting nature, they make a successful and formidable partnership.

In the parent–child relationship the Rat child thrives on the love and attentiveness of a Pig parent as well as appreciating the secure and harmonious atmosphere of a Pig home. There is a close and enduring bond between them. When the Rat is parent and Pig the child, relations between these signs are again good. The Rat parent provides the love, support and discipline that helps to bring out the positive qualities in a Pig child and there is much love between them. In both combinations the parents and children of these signs relate well to each other and the children gain and learn much from their parents.

In Love and Marriage

There is considerable attraction between the Rat and Pig and, in love and marriage, they can find much happiness. Both are passionate and sensual signs and there is a strong physical attraction between them. They understand each other well and share many interests.

Both the Rat and Pig have lively and outgoing natures and have a fondness for the good things in life. They both like socializing and partying and generally live and enjoy life to the full.

They are both home-oriented signs and attach much importance to their home and family. They make caring and attentive parents and devote much time and energy in bringing up any children they have. They also put a great deal of energy into creating and maintaining their home and between them make sure it is tastefully and comfortably furnished and that it possesses a homely and harmonious atmosphere. Their home may, however, quickly become full; with the Pig's indulgence and the Rat's acquisitive and hoarding nature, they could have more possessions than they know what to do with.

Between them the Rat and Pig have considerable earning ability; most Rat–Pig couples are financially secure and able to enjoy a good standard of living.

There is considerable empathy between these two signs and a great deal of love. The Rat particularly values the Pig's affectionate, sincere and good-natured manner as well as appreciating his talents as a money-maker, while the Pig will delight in the versatility, resourcefulness, charm and wit of the Rat. They make super companions and in love and marriage are ideally suited. An excellent match.

OX AND OX

General Relations

There is respect and admiration between two Oxen but not always close friendship. Oxen are resolute, ambitious and often loners and while one Ox may recognize the qualities and tenacity in another Ox, they often prefer to keep their distance. Each Ox cherishes his independence and each likes to have his own way; when two Oxen come together it may well mean a clash of interests and a struggle for dominance. General relations between two Oxen can be reasonable, but no more.

Where possible, the Ox likes to work independently of others and be free to set about his duties in his own way and own style. However, should he find himself working with another Ox, either as a colleague or business partner, it is possible that they may combine their talents and enjoy success. Both will be hard and tenacious workers and if they are united in achieving a particular goal their perseverance and determination is invariably rewarded. In a working relationship between two Oxen it might be best if there is a clear division of responsibilities, otherwise there may be a tussle for authority. However, Oxen are disciplined workers and their ambitious and strong-willed natures can make them a powerful force.

In the parent–child relationship an Ox child thrives in a secure and stable Ox home. The conscientious Ox parent provides discipline and expert guidance for the Ox child and the child strives to please his parent. There is a good bond between them although the Ox child's stubbornness may cause the occasional rift. Generally, though, they understand each other well and while neither may be over-demonstrative in their affection, they love each other dearly.

In Love and Marriage

The Ox chooses his friends carefully and it often takes him some time before he feels totally at ease with another. The Ox is well placed to understand another Ox, however, and if both are seeking romance there may be a considerable attraction between them.

Both Oxen seek a secure, stable and calm lifestyle. Neither likes change or lots of activity and with their joint interests – particularly their fondness for gardening, the countryside and outdoor life – they may find a certain contentment. As a couple they will conduct their activities in an orderly and efficient manner and as neither have expensive tastes most Ox couples are materially well off. Both also have practical natures and an Ox couple take much delight in creating and maintaining their home.

There is also a great deal of trust between them. The Ox is loyal and faithful and keenly aware of his responsibilities. If Oxen have children they make conscientious, caring, but also strict, parents.

An Ox couple can form a satisfactory match but there may be problems they will need to address. Both can be strong willed and stubborn and each likes to have his own way. They may find compromise difficult and as each can be forthright there may be some very frank exchanges between them. Also, Oxen tend to be set in their ways and a relationship between two Oxen may be devoid of excitement, zest or sparkle. With their serious natures there may be a distinct lack of lightheartedness or frivolity in an Ox household.

However, while there may be difficulties and problems for an

Ox couple, they do understand each other. Each is conscientious, dutiful and works hard. They may not always agree but they love, respect and admire each other. In love and marriage a relationship between two Oxen can work, but it does need care and understanding.

Ox and Tiger

General Relations

The Ox and Tiger are two forceful and determined signs and their personalities and temperaments simply clash. Neither finds it easy to relate to the other and general relations between them are poor. The practical and down-to-earth Ox finds the Tiger too restless and volatile, while the Tiger views the Ox as unadventurous, intractable and too set in his ways. They have few interests in common and there is a distinct lack of understanding between them.

The differences in personality are also evident when they work together. The Tiger, often bubbling with enthusiasm and new ideas, finds the cautious Ox far too much of a restraining and inhibiting influence, while the Ox considers the Tiger rash, reckless and impulsive. Their attitudes and outlooks are often so different that agreement and understanding between them is hard to attain. Both signs clash and are likely to go their separate ways.

In the parent–child relationship relations between these two signs also need careful handling. The Tiger parent may admire the dutiful and conscientious nature of the Ox child, but the child may feel ill at ease with the parent's restless and volatile nature. The Ox child prefers a calm and stable atmosphere rather than the constant level of activity that so often exists in a Tiger household. When the Ox is parent and Tiger the child, the Ox parent may marvel at the Tiger child's enterprise and versatility but could despair over the child's ebullient and strong-minded ways. In both cases there are times when their resolute and stubborn natures clash and, despite their best endeavours, relations between parent and child are never easy.

In Love and Marriage

Although these two signs have many fine and admirable qualities they do not find it easy to get on well together and, in love and marriage, a match between them may prove both difficult and challenging.

It is possible that, for a time, the Ox may be attracted to the Tiger's vibrant and engaging personality and the Tiger may admire the calm, sincere and dependable nature of the Ox, but any feelings that they have for each other may be difficult to maintain. In terms of temperament there is a wide gulf between them.

The Ox prefers to set about his activities in a calm, methodical and orderly manner. Often conservative in outlook, he tends to have specific interests, seeks stability and does not like change. The Tiger, however, is far more adventurous and outgoing than the Ox. He revels in challenges and new situations and indulges in a wide range of activities. The Tiger enjoys action and has an enterprising and somewhat restless nature. The Ox and Tiger live life at different speeds and in different ways. Agreement between them is difficult and neither shows much willingness to adapt to the other.

They have few interests in common. The Tiger likes to lead an active social life, while the Ox is not a great socializer. The Tiger is passionate and seeks fun and, while the Ox too enjoys life in his own way, he tends not to be as outgoing as the Tiger and is far more serious and restrained in his manner. Similarly, there are disagreements in money matters. The Ox tends to be prudent and cautious, while the Tiger often spends his money freely and, to the Ox, appears over generous and too indulgent.

Both signs can be stubborn and strong willed and, with their different outlooks, there are likely to be many disagreements and clashes between them. In love and marriage the Ox and Tiger are ill suited and it takes an exceptional couple to make the relationship work.

Ox and Rabbit

General Relations

The Ox and Rabbit admire each other and can become firm and loyal friends. Both prefer the quieter things in life and have many interests they can share. They relate well to each other and there is a good level of trust and understanding between them. General relations between these two signs are invariably good.

The Ox and Rabbit also work well together. Both are methodical, diligent and conscientious workers and they like to plan their activities well and carefully. In a business relationship each benefits from the other. The Rabbit values the strength, tenacity and resolution of the Ox, while the Ox appreciates the shrewd business sense and commercial acumen of the Rabbit. They trust and support each other well. Admittedly neither are big risk-takers and both are conservative in outlook, but their joint skills usually bring them much success.

In the parent–child relationship the genial and well-behaved Rabbit child is a delight for the Ox parent and there is much love and understanding between them. The Rabbit child truly values the strength and support of an Ox parent and gains and learns much from the parent. When the Rabbit is parent and Ox the child, the dutiful Ox child again responds well to a kindly Rabbit parent and thrives in the secure and settled atmosphere of a Rabbit home. There is a good bond between them.

In Love and Marriage

There is considerable attraction between the Ox and Rabbit and in love and marriage they can find much happiness.

Although there are many personality differences between them – the Ox being more assertive and strong willed than the Rabbit – they complement each other well and each values and gains from the other's strengths. The Rabbit delights in having such a resolute, dependable and protective partner, while the Ox values the thoughtful, intelligent and affectionate ways of the Rabbit. They relate well to each other and share similar views and outlooks. They are both quiet and peaceloving signs and neither wants to pursue a particularly frenzied or volatile lifestyle. They both value their home life and are most supportive and attentive to each other. They also have interests that they can share. Both appreciate music, literature and the arts and may have a fondness for the countryside.

With their methodical and conscientious natures, they each have the skill to earn a great deal and, as both tend to be careful in money matters, most Ox–Rabbit couples are materially well off.

The Ox may not be so keen a socializer as the Rabbit and the sensitive Rabbit may sometimes be unsettled by the Ox's forthright nature, but both these signs make every effort to adapt to each other. In love and marriage each gains much from their relationship and together the Ox and Rabbit find much happiness and contentment. An ideal match.

OX AND DRAGON

General Relations

Although the Ox and Dragon may admire and respect each other they rarely become close friends. Both appreciate each other's honest and forthright natures and each possesses much integrity. However, the Dragon is an extrovert, always active and a keen socializer. The Ox is quieter, more of a loner and lives life at a totally different speed to the Dragon. They have few interests in common and each prefers spending time with those more in tune with his own interests and personalities.

Relations between the Ox and Dragon improve when they work together, either as colleagues or business partners. Both are ambitious and diligent workers and each recognizes the qualities in the other. The Ox values the enterprise and enthusiasm of the Dragon, while the Dragon appreciates the tenacity and persistence of the Ox. When they are united in a common objective the Ox and Dragon make a formidable team. However, given that both are forceful characters, it is best if they each have a clear division of responsibilities; otherwise there may be much jockeying for control.

In the parent–child relationship relations between these two signs need to be handled with care. The Ox parent is proud of the Dragon child's versatility and keenness to learn, but may not be too tolerant of the Dragon child's high-spirited and independent-minded ways. When the Dragon is parent and Ox the child, the quiet and dutiful Ox child may feel ill at ease with his lively and extrovert Dragon parent and relations between them could prove difficult. The Ox child seeks a calm and orderly existence and this is not always possible with a vibrant and enterprising Dragon about.

In Love and Marriage

The Ox and Dragon each have qualities that the other admires and for a time they may be attracted to each other. The Dragon values the sincerity, calmness and stable manner of the Ox, while the Ox admires the zest, energy and enthusiasm of the Dragon. Each enjoys being with an opposite – an introvert exploring the world of an extrovert and vice versa. They are also both honest and forthright and each has a trusting nature. Both are keen and diligent workers and again each recognizes the abilities of the other.

However, despite any initial attraction between the Ox and Dragon, the long-term prospects for their relationship are difficult.

Both the Ox and Dragon are forceful characters and each may try to dominate the relationship. They can also both be stubborn and their forthright natures may lead to many frank and heated exchanges. They also have different interests. The Dragon likes to lead an active social life and engages in a wide variety of activities, while the Ox prefers a much gentler existence. He does not share in the Dragon's desire for a lot of socializing or being constantly on the go; he much prefers spending time quietly at home. The Dragon may feel restricted by the Ox, while the Ox may feel unsettled by the activity and restlessness of the Dragon. Their forceful natures cause friction between them and their different interests pull them apart.

In love and marriage relations between the Ox and Dragon are far from easy. Their personalities, interests and outlooks are so very different that these two strong-willed signs will ultimately just clash. A difficult match.

Ox and Snake

General Relations

These two signs have much in common and general relations between them are good. Both have quiet and reserved natures and feel comfortable in each other's company. There is trust and understanding between them and they relate well to each other. The Ox admires the Snake's thoughtful and reflective ways, while the Snake values the Ox's caring, confident and determined nature. They respect each other and may become firm and loyal friends.

The Ox and Snake also work well together and by combining their different strengths, they create a strong force to be reckoned with. Both are ambitious and both are keen to make the most of their considerable talents. The Snake in particular values the tenacity, willpower and determination of the Ox, while the Ox values the Snake's keen business sense and often original ideas. They trust and respect each other and, as colleagues or business partners, make a successful combination.

In the parent–child relationship the Snake child loves and respects his Ox parent dearly and there is a good rapport between them. The Ox parent does much to guide and encourage the Snake child and the Snake child responds well to the Ox parent's quiet, firm and dependable nature. When the Snake is parent and Ox the child, the Snake parent may admire the dutiful ways of the Ox child, but the Ox child's sometimes stubborn nature may cause problems between them. For the most part, however, relations between them are good and the Ox child strives to please his thoughtful and reflective parent.

In Love and Marriage

These two signs are often attracted to each other and in love and marriage they make a good match.

Both the Ox and Snake are generally quiet and placid signs and often have many interests in common. The Ox greatly admires the Snake's discreet and thoughtful manner, his cultivated tastes and good humour. The Ox also values the Snake's opinions as well as being captivated by the Snake's magnetic charm.

Similarly, the Snake values the Ox's practical and dependable nature. The Ox is hard working, resolute and ambitious. He knows what he wants in life and such an attitude finds favour with an equally ambitious Snake. The Snake feels inspired and yet secure in the company of a caring and considerate Ox.

The Ox is a splendid homemaker and quite often the Snake prefers to leave many of the decisions and domestic arrangements in the capable hands of the Ox, while the Snake takes charge of their finances and paperwork. As a couple they work very much as a team, with each benefiting from the skills and strengths of the other. There is much trust and loyalty between them.

As a couple they also enjoy many joint interests. Both may have an appreciation of the arts, particularly music and literature, and also outdoor activities such as walking and exploring the countryside. The Ox and Snake are well suited to each other and, if they have a family, they make caring and responsible parents.

Although some may find these two signs rather distant and aloof, the Ox and Snake understand each other well. There is a good rapport between them and in love and marriage they can find much happiness. An often excellent and fulfilling match.

Ox and Horse

General Relations

The Ox and Horse are two strong-willed and strong-minded signs; relations between them will be difficult. They share few interests and their different personalities often lead them in opposite directions. The Horse likes to lead an active and energetic lifestyle and is a keen socializer, while the Ox is quieter, more reserved and seeks a stabler existence. There is little rapport and understanding between them and general relations between these two signs are often poor.

Although the Ox and Horse may both be industrious and work hard, they do not work well together. The Ox is careful, methodical and cautious, while the Horse is far more adventurous and enterprising. Their resolute natures and different outlooks could lead to many disagreements between them. If the Ox and Horse can unite for a common objective it is possible they may usefully combine their different strengths, but generally they are likely to go their own way and rely on their own methods rather than co-operate or work closely together.

In the parent–child relationship problems between these two signs can again emerge. The caring and dutiful Ox parent may delight in the Horse child's intelligence and versatility, but could find the Horse child self-willed and over-independent. The Ox parent, who as a child so valued the security of his home, finds it hard to understand the restlessness of the Horse or that the Horse child wishes to leave home so young. When the Horse is parent and Ox the child, the Horse parent again admires the diligence of the Ox child but the Ox child feels ill at ease with the bustle and activity that so often exists in a Horse household. The Ox child craves for a quiet and tranquil existence and understanding between Horse parent and Ox child may prove difficult.

In Love and Marriage

The Ox and Horse do not generally relate well to each other. They have few interests in common and often prefer to set about their activities in different ways. However, it is possible that despite their many differences each sign may be attracted by the strengths and qualities in the other. The Ox may enjoy the wit, intelligence and affection of the Horse, while the Horse admires the integrity and loyalty of the Ox. Each may learn and gain from the other, but in love and marriage they need to overcome many obstacles if they are to form a lasting and harmonious relationship.

Both the Ox and Horse can be strong willed. Each may try to dominate the relationship and, given their stubborn natures, they may not always find it easy to compromise. Also both tend to live life at different speeds. The Horse likes to keep himself active, have a wide range of interests and lead a busy social life, while the Ox prefers a quieter, calmer and more orderly existence. The Horse is constantly wanting to go out, while the Ox prefers the comforts of home. Similarly, the Horse wishes to retain a certain independence and freedom in his actions, which the Ox may find difficult to understand. Both can also be forthright in their views and, as each has a temper, there could be many heated exchanges between them. Their different personalities, interests and outlooks do not make for easy living.

The Horse is a romantic and may not find the Ox as passionate or as outgoing in his affections as he may like.

The Ox and Horse both possess many admirable qualities, but their personalities are generally not suited to each other. In love and marriage this can prove a difficult and challenging match.

Ox and Goat

General Relations

The Ox and Goat have little in common and general relations between them are poor. The hard-working, conscientious and dutiful Ox has little appreciation of the Goat's imaginative, whimsical and often carefree nature and is irritated by the Goat's capriciousness. The Goat in turn finds the Ox too serious and matter of fact. The Goat likes socializing, while the Ox is more a loner. There is little understanding between the two signs and rarely do they become friends.

The Ox and Goat also have different attitudes to their work and, when they are colleagues or business partners, relations again prove difficult. The Ox is a hard and diligent worker and he sets about his activities with considerable determination and willpower. The Goat, however, just does not have the tenacity or the ambition of the Ox and, while the Goat may admire the Ox's commitment, there is little understanding between them. The Ox despairs of the Goat's sometimes hesitant and indecisive nature, while the Goat finds the Ox intransigent and at times obstinate. In a working situation their personalities and outlooks often clash.

In the parent–child relationship, when the Goat is parent and Ox the child, the Goat parent may find it hard to relate to the serious and dutiful Ox child. The Ox child does not share the joyful and imaginative nature of the Goat parent and there may be few grounds of common interest. Try as they may, relations between them are difficult. When the Ox is parent and Goat the child, the Goat child can, however, gain much from an Ox parent. The Ox parent, while firm, encourages his children with their many interests and while he may not fully understand the artistic and imaginative world of the Goat child, at least the Goat child feels secure and protected by having such a resolute and dependable parent.

In Love and Marriage

The Ox and Goat have very different personalities and relations between them can prove difficult. For a time the Ox may enjoy the genial and affectionate nature of the Goat and the Goat may value the strength, confidence and sincerity of the Ox, but they may find it hard to maintain their affection for each other.

In many ways the Ox and Goat are opposites. The Ox is careful, dutiful and methodical in his attitude, while the Goat is more easygoing. The Goat lives for the moment and is capricious, while the Ox is decisive, plans his activities with care and is not one for sudden changes. The Ox is soon exasperated by the Goat's carefree attitude, while the Goat finds the Ox intolerant, demanding and too serious. The Ox also does not fully appreciate the Goat's artistic and imaginative nature, while the more sensitive Goat feels ill at ease with the Ox's forthright manner.

There may also be differences over money. The Ox is careful with money, while the Goat tends to spend his freely.

If the Ox and Goat are able to go some way towards reconciling their many differences, they may learn much from each other. The Goat may gain in confidence and become more organized and disciplined, while the Ox may become more relaxed and more appreciative of the finer things in life. However, there is a wide gulf between them and it takes an exceptional couple to make this relationship work. In love and marriage this is a difficult and challenging match.

Ox and Monkey

General Relations

The Ox and Monkey have a mutual respect for each other, although on a purely social level each may prefer signs more like themselves. The Monkey has a lively and outgoing nature and likes to lead an active social life, while the Ox is quieter, tends to take life more seriously and is not a great socializer. However, despite their character differences, both recognize qualities in the other and, for the most part, can get on well together without necessarily becoming close friends.

When the Ox and Monkey work together, either as colleagues or business partners, they can make a successful team, with each complementing the skills of the other. The Ox values the Monkey's resourcefulness and quick thinking, while the Monkey gains much from the Ox's more practical and persistent approach. The more cautious Ox also acts as a stabilizing influence on the Monkey, while the Ox benefits from the Monkey's inventiveness. Both are ambitious, both are astute and, although there may be essential character differences between them, they have a good respect and regard for each other.

In a parent–child relationship the Ox parent delights in the Monkey child's versatility and keenness to learn and relations between them are good, even though the Ox parent may not always appreciate the Monkey child's pranks! When the Monkey is parent and Ox the child, relations may be a little more tricky. The quiet and dutiful Ox child may find it hard to relate to a lively Monkey parent, but if the Monkey parent can instil some humour into the Ox child and make the child more outgoing this is very much in the Ox child's interests. With care and understanding they can develop a sound and loving relationship.

In Love and Marriage

For all their many differences, the Ox and Monkey are often attracted to each other and in love and marriage they can make a good match. Each appreciates the qualities found in the other and their different characters and strengths complement each other admirably.

The Ox has the discipline and tenacity that the Monkey often lacks and can be a steadying influence on the Monkey. The Ox gives the Monkey a sense of security and stability as well as being loyal and dependable. The Monkey, too, appreciates the sincerity and unpretentiousness of the Ox.

Similarly, the Ox can gain much from the Monkey. The Monkey makes lively and enjoyable company and this can be a tonic for the quiet and dutiful Ox. The Ox may become more outgoing under the Monkey's influence as well as broadening his interests and outlook. The Monkey shows the Ox how to enjoy life more rather than to wrap himself up in his own individual concerns and activities. Admittedly the Ox may not always enjoy such an active lifestyle as the Monkey likes to lead but both are respectful of the other.

In their relationship there is a good understanding between them and each is devoted to the other. If they have children both make caring and conscientious parents and the children benefit from the different qualities found in an introverted and extroverted parent.

The Ox and Monkey make a good match. They complement each other well and in love and marriage can find much contentment. Both gain much from their relationship.

Ox and Rooster

General Relations

These two signs get on well together and can become firm friends. They respect and admire each other and often share similar interests. The Rooster admires the calm, sincere and determined manner of the Ox, while the Ox finds the Rooster, with his many interests and outgoing nature, stimulating company. Both are methodical and set themselves high standards. There is a good rapport and understanding between them and general relations between the Ox and Rooster are invariably good.

The Ox and Rooster also work well together, either as colleagues or business partners. They recognize each other's strengths and there is much trust and respect between them. Each motivates and encourages the other. The Ox gains from the Rooster's organizational talents and more outgoing nature, while the Rooster is inspired by the Ox's tenacity and willpower. Both are efficient and methodical in their duties and make a powerful and often successful combination.

In the parent–child relationship relations again are excellent. The Rooster parent admires the conscientiousness and tenacity of the Ox child and does much to encourage the Ox child in his various activities. The Ox child strives to please his Rooster parent and values the sense of order and routine that exists in a Rooster household. When the Ox is parent and Rooster the child, the Rooster child relates well to the Ox parent, valuing the Ox parent's attentiveness and admiring his purposeful and resolute manner. The Ox parent sets a fine example for the Rooster child; an example the child will be keen to emulate. In both combinations there is a good rapport between parent and child.

In Love and Marriage

The Ox and Rooster are often attracted to each other and are ideally suited. They share similar values and outlooks and they complement each other extremely well. Both are practical, well organized and methodical. There is a good understanding and rapport between them and in love and marriage they can find much happiness.

As a couple they work as a team, each helping and supporting the other. Together they spend much time on their joint interests; both may be keen gardeners and enjoy the countryside and nature as well as being avid readers. They also devote considerable energy to their home and to any children that they have. Both make conscientious parents.

They also benefit from each other's individual strengths. The Rooster helps to make the Ox more outgoing as well as broadening his interests, while the Ox is a steadying influence on the Rooster's sometimes volatile nature. Both are conservative in outlook, both are practical and both are keen to make the most of their considerable abilities. Admittedly they can be forthright in expressing their views but each admires the frankness and honesty in the other. They respect each other's views and judgement.

The Ox and Rooster complement each other well and in love and marriage can form an excellent and lasting relationship; a relationship founded on love, loyalty and trust.

Ox and Dog

General Relations

Although the Ox and Dog may admire each other's open, sincere and dependable natures their outlooks and personalities often clash. Both signs can be forthright and stubborn and they share few interests in common. The Ox's domineering attitude may be resented by the Dog, while the Dog's idealism is not fully appreciated by the Ox. Relations between these signs can be fair, but they may have difficulty in building up a satisfactory rapport.

Similarly when the Ox and Dog work together, either as colleagues or business partners, relations again may prove difficult. The Ox is ambitious, tenacious and eager to give of his best and he has little patience with the Dog's worrying and sometimes pessimistic tendencies. The Ox does not share the Dog's idealism or approve of the Dog's generous and spendthrift ways. The Dog, in turn, may resent the Ox's authoritarian and intransigent attitude. In work there will be a lack of trust and understanding between them.

In the parent–child relationship relations between these two signs will need to be handled with care. While the Ox parent loves, encourages and supports the Dog child, he may not fully appreciate the Dog's sensitive nature or be as demonstrative in his affections as the Dog child would like. When the Dog is parent and Ox the child, the Dog parent will admire the responsible and diligent nature of the Ox child, but both parent and child can be forthright and stubborn and there are times when relations between them are far from easy.

In Love and Marriage

The Ox and Dog may be attracted by each other's more positive qualities, but relations between them may sometimes be difficult. In love and marriage this may be a challenging, but not impossible, match.

Both these signs share an important quality – loyalty – and both are faithful to their partner. The Dog admires the confident and determined nature of the Ox as well as appreciating the Ox's sincere and dependable manner. Similarly, the Ox values the affection, support and discretion of the Dog. Each trusts the other, but understanding between them may not always be easy.

Although the Ox may admire the Dog's selfless nature, he is not as idealistic as the Dog nor will he be as sensitive with regard to the Dog's worrying and pessimistic nature. The Dog in turn, may find the Ox intransigent and too commanding in attitude. The practical and down-to-earth Ox may not always be as spontaneous or as warm in his affections as the Dog may like. However if the Ox and the Dog are prepared to make the effort it is possible that they can form a meaningful relationship and indeed gain from each other. The anxious Dog may benefit from the Ox's confident manner, while the Dog may help the Ox broaden his interests and make him more sociable. Also, as both attach such importance to their home life, they may pour much time and energy into their home and any children that they have.

In love and marriage a relationship between the Ox and Dog may just work, but it may not be easy and a lot of compromising and adjusting is necessary.

Ox and Pig

General Relations

There is much respect between the Ox and Pig and these two signs can become firm friends. The Ox likes the sincerity and openness of the Pig, while the Pig admires the integrity and dutiful nature of the Ox. They relate well to each other and there is a good understanding between them. Although the Ox may not be such a keen socializer as the Pig, they do share many interests and both may have a particular interest in gardening, the countryside and outdoor life. General relations between these two signs are good.

The Ox and Pig also work well together. Both are persistent and diligent workers and once committed to a certain objective they work long and hard to achieve their goal. They are patient and tenacious and there is much respect and loyalty between them. The Ox gains from the Pig's enterprise and the Pig from the Ox's methodical manner and, by combining their skills, they may enjoy considerable success.

In the parent–child relationship relations between these signs are again good. The calm, thoughtful and caring Ox sets a shining example to his children and the Pig child responds well to the Ox parent and strives to please. There is much love and respect between them. When the Pig is parent and Ox the child, the Pig parent does much to encourage the dutiful Ox child as well as helping him to become more relaxed and outgoing. In both combinations the children learn much from their parents.

In Love and Marriage

The Ox and Pig are often attracted to each other and together can build a successful relationship. There is much love and loyalty between them and each gains from the other.

Both the Ox and Pig are open and honest in their feelings and there is considerable trust between them. They are both hard-working and conscientious and between them they enjoy a stable and comfortable way of life. They both value their home and devote much time and energy into creating a comfortable and secure base. Both have practical natures and are constantly undertaking DIY projects or have some activity under way. They also have a fondness for the outdoor life and both the Ox and Pig can be keen gardeners, enjoy rambling or just being in the countryside. The main difference between them, however, is that the Pig enjoys a much more active social life than the Ox and there are times when the Pig may wish the Ox were more outgoing.

However, there is considerable empathy between these two signs and each strives to please the other. They also benefit from each other's personalities. The serious and dutiful Ox may become more relaxed and easygoing under the Pig's genial influence, while the Pig may become more discerning, less indulgent and better organized.

In love and marriage the Ox and Pig mean much to each other. They both share similar values and outlooks and both are mindful of their duties and responsibilities. They are well suited and make a good match.

TIGER AND TIGER

General Relations

With his lively and outgoing nature the Tiger makes friends with ease. However, when it comes to his own kind relations are difficult. The Tiger is bold, forthright and likes to have his own way. When two Tigers come together they clash. Each tries to dominate the other and any sort of understanding between them is difficult. Tigers are also independent minded and neither really needs another strong-willed Tiger for companionship. General relations between two Tigers are invariably poor.

Similarly, should two Tigers find themselves working together, relations between them will again prove difficult. The Tiger likes to lead and dominate and each wants their own way. They are also both competitive and, rather than pooling their resources and working as a team, they are more likely to end up competing against each other. They are too restless and too independent minded for any satisfactory working relationship to exist. As colleagues or business partners two Tigers will quickly go their own way.

In the parent–child relationship the attentive Tiger parent is keen to encourage his resourceful Tiger child and the child learns much from the parent. However, the Tiger child is strong willed and has a mind of his own and there are times when he will clash with his equally strong-minded parent. Even though their relations may not always be easy, there is still much love between them.

In Love and Marriage

Vibrant, exciting and enterprising, the Tiger makes marvellous company. He is lively and sociable and has a passionate and amorous nature. When two Tigers meet they may have much fun together, but the attraction between them could be short lived. In love and marriage this can be a difficult match.

The Tiger is proud, dominant and likes to have his own way. In a relationship between two Tigers each will want to dominate and there could be constant tussles for authority. They are also both forthright in their views and this may give rise to many heated exchanges.

Tigers like to retain a certain independence in their actions and this, too, could put a strain on their relationship. Each wants to do his own thing in his own way and in time this desire for independence may become more pronounced. A Tiger couple can also be restless and there may be a distinct lack of stability in a Tiger household. Also, both tend to spend their money freely and, without care, together they may quickly deplete any savings they might have.

Generally, although Tigers have many fine and admirable qualities, they are ill suited for each other. They are too dominant, too headstrong and too restless to live in harmony and it takes an exceptional Tiger couple to make this relationship work.

TIGER AND RABBIT

General Relations

The Tiger and Rabbit find each other interesting company. The Rabbit admires the Tiger's courage, zest and enthusiasm, while the Tiger values the Rabbit's discreet and companionable nature. Although they have very different personalities – the Tiger being far more outgoing and adventurous than the Rabbit – they respect each other and general relations between these two signs are reasonably good.

When the Tiger and Rabbit work together each benefits from the skills and strengths of the other. The Rabbit gains from the enthusiastic, enterprising and innovative nature of the Tiger, while the Tiger benefits from the planning, organizational skills and sound business sense of the Rabbit. The Rabbit also acts as a valuable restraining influence on some of the Tiger's more reckless notions. By combining their different skills they can make a fine team, although it is best if the more prudent Rabbit controls the financial aspects of any concern.

In the parent–child relationship the dutiful and compliant Rabbit child will be a delight to the Tiger parent and the Tiger parent does much to encourage the child. However, the Rabbit child may sometimes feel ill at ease with the bustle and general level of activity in a Tiger household. When the Rabbit is parent and Tiger the child, the Rabbit parent will encourage the Tiger child's inquisitive nature and thirst for knowledge, but at the same time be troubled by the child's independent-minded and sometimes stubborn nature. Although, in both cases, relations need to be handled with care, there is still much love between parent and child.

In Love and Marriage

There is considerable attraction between the Tiger and Rabbit. The Rabbit delights in the lively, vivacious and confident nature of the Tiger, while the Tiger values the Rabbit's discreet, refined and sociable manner. Both are also passionate and sensual signs and there is a strong physical attraction between them.

They are both keen socializers as well as creatures of comfort and enjoy leading an active social life, entertaining their wide circle of friends as well as devoting much time and energy to their home. They also gain from each other's company. The Rabbit may become more assertive under the Tiger's influence, while the Tiger may become better organized, more prudent and less impulsive. The Rabbit also acts as a steadying influence on the Tiger's restless nature. Together the Tiger and Rabbit will support each other well and there is a good element of fun and understanding between them.

However, if they are to maintain their close relationship each needs to show some willingness to adjust to the other. The Rabbit needs to allow the Tiger a certain independence and freedom in his actions rather than insist on complete together-ness in everything they do, while the Tiger needs to be respectful of the Rabbit's feelings. Sometimes the Tiger's adventurous and forthright nature can prove unsettling for the more sensitive and security-conscious Rabbit. However, despite the differences between them, they appreciate each other's finer qualities and, providing they are prepared to adapt to each other, in love and marriage they can form a satisfying and fulfilling match.

Tiger and Dragon

General Relations

The Tiger and Dragon may enjoy each other's company for a time; both like to keep themselves active, enjoy socializing and travelling and may also share a fondness for outdoor activities. But both are strong-willed signs and both like to have their own way. In time their dominant and forceful personalities may clash, particularly as both can be so forthright when expressing their views and opinions. General relations between these two signs can be good but are often volatile.

In a working situation the Tiger and Dragon can make an effective combination. Both are enterprising and ambitious and between them they have a never-ending supply of ideas and projects to pursue. They are also risk takers and can be bold and resourceful in their actions. Providing they do not overreach themselves or let their impulsive natures get the better of them they can enjoy considerable success. As colleagues or business partners they make a fine and dynamic duo.

In the parent–child relationship relations between these signs are again good. Both Tiger and Dragon parents delight in the zest, keenness and intelligence of a Tiger or Dragon child and do much to support and encourage the child. The Tiger or Dragon child in turn values the love, liveliness and enterprise of the parent and aims to live up to the parent's expectations. The main problem emerges when the child challenges the parent's word or proves stubborn over a certain matter. Both Tiger and Dragon parents demand and expect obedience and when this is not forthcoming, tempers fly. However, despite the occasional and almost inevitable clash between them, parent–child relationships between these two signs are founded on much love and respect.

In Love and Marriage

With their lively, passionate and outgoing natures, the Tiger and Dragon are often attracted to each other. In the early days of their relationship there is passion – lots of passion – fun, excitement and times of great happiness. Both are also great optimists and, with their enterprising natures, they are capable of devising many wonderful plans for the future. Life in a Dragon–Tiger household is certainly never dull!

As a couple they also have interests they can share. Both are keen socializers and travellers and both like to keep themselves occupied with a wide range of activities. However, while there is so much in favour of a relationship between these two active and enterprising signs, there are also problems they need to address.

Both the Tiger and Dragon are forceful signs and like to have their own way. Unless there is a clear division of responsibilities, each may try to dominate the relationship. Both can be too forthright in their views and while each admires openness in the other, their frankness may lead to some heated exchanges. The Tiger and Dragon can also be restless and crave for a certain independence in their actions and this may put a strain on their relationship. Similarly, their impulsive, impatient and sometimes reckless natures may lead to friction between them.

If the Tiger and Dragon are prepared to compromise over disagreements and allow each other a certain independence in their actions then they may be able to sustain the intensity of the early glorious days of their relationship. If not, their strongwilled and domineering personalities will bring them into conflict. In love and marriage this can be a challenging, but certainly not impossible, match.

Tiger and Snake

General Relations

The Tiger and Snake do not relate well to each other. The Tiger is a strong-minded extrovert, while the Snake is a strong-minded introvert. The Snake is calm, orderly and reflective, while the Tiger is full of energy, vigour and verve. Neither feels disposed to make much effort to understand the other and, apart from a once in a while lively discussion, these two signs prefer to socialize with others more in tune with their own character, attitudes and interests. General relations between them are poor.

For any business relationship to work there has to be trust and this may well be lacking when the Tiger and Snake find themselves as colleagues or business partners. The Snake considers the Tiger reckless, volatile and a spendthrift, while the Tiger is suspicious of the Snake's quiet, guarded and sometimes secretive nature. The Tiger is impulsive and action orientated while the Snake is more patient and calculating. The Snake does not like to be hurried and the Tiger is constantly in a hurry. If the two signs are prepared to go some way towards reconciling their differences, the Tiger and Snake may find each other benefiting from the other's strengths – the bold Tiger spurring the Snake into action, while the Snake brings method, consistency and financial acumen to the Tiger's actions. But as both signs find it hard to like or trust the other, rarely does this happen.

This lack of rapport is also evident in a parent–child relationship. When the Tiger is the parent and Snake the child, the Tiger parent may find it hard to accept or understand the quiet, withdrawn and reflective manner of a Snake child. Similarly the Snake child may feel ill at ease with the general hustle and bustle that exists in a Tiger household. The Snake child yearns for a peaceful and orderly existence. When the Snake is parent and the Tiger child, the Snake parent could find it hard to cope with the exuberance, flamboyance and independent-mindedness of a Tiger child. Relations between them are difficult.

In Love and Marriage

Tradition does not bode well for a match between these two signs. Admittedly there may be some initial attraction between them – the Tiger being enchanted by the quiet and seductive ways of the Snake and the Snake by the Tiger's lively and personable nature – but any attraction is likely to be short-lived. In many ways the Tiger and Snake are opposites and generally do not get on well.

Tigers are action-orientated souls who like to enjoy and live life to the full. The Snake, however, is calm, reflective and sets about life at his own pace and in his own way. The Snake just cannot accept the bustle and vigour with which the Tiger chooses to conduct his activities, while the Tiger quickly loses patience with the slow and calculating ways of the Snake.

The Tiger also resents the possessiveness of a Snake partner. The Tiger likes to retain a certain independence in his actions and to be reasonably free to do as he chooses and the Snake views such an attitude with misgivings and mistrust – the Snake does so like to keep tabs on his partner. Also, as the Tiger tends to spend more freely than the Snake, there may be conflicts over money matters.

The Tiger and Snake share few interests and, with rare exceptions, neither sign is prepared to make the radical adjustments needed to suit the other. Should the Tiger and Snake fall in love and marry, the path ahead may prove difficult.

TIGER AND HORSE

General Relations

The Tiger and Horse are two lively and spirited individuals who get on well together. They share many interests, including a love of discussion, travel and the great outdoors and with their enthusiasm and boundless energy they will have many good times together. They enjoy each other's company and there is a good rapport between them. The Tiger and Horse often become firm friends.

These two signs also work well together and, as colleagues or business partners, can enjoy considerable success. Both are bold, enterprising and work hard. Neither is afraid of taking risks and between them they are likely to devise many interesting and unusual projects. They trust and respect each other and while each can at times be volatile and reckless it is hoped that the other will exercise a restraining influence. With their enthusiasm, determination and faith in their abilities, the Tiger and Horse make an awe-inspiring combination.

The parent–child relationship between these signs is again good. In this relationship it does not matter if the Tiger is parent and the Horse the child or vice versa; both share similar characteristics. Tiger and Horse children are outgoing, energetic and keen to learn. They are also strong willed and can be stubborn – both of which lead to inevitable conflicts with their parents – but the Tiger and Horse parent recognize and nurture the positive qualities in their offspring and there is much love and respect between them. As both Tiger and Horse children have an independent streak in them it is likely that they choose to leave home early, but there is always a lasting bond between the parents and children of these two signs.

In Love and Marriage

The Tiger and Horse are both passionate and sensual signs and, with their good looks and lively personalities, they are often attracted to each other. There is a good understanding and rapport between them and together they will have fun, excitement and live life to the full.

They share many interests, are keen socializers and both possess an adventurous spirit. However, what is particularly important in this match is that, despite their loyalty and devotion to one another, each recognizes that the other still needs a certain independence and does not insist on complete togetherness in everything they do. Both the Tiger and the Horse feel a necessity to have some freedom and appreciate the ability to go off and devote time to their own interests. They enjoy togetherness but they also both value their freedom and independence.

The Tiger and Horse also hold strong opinions, are frank in exchanging their views and can be stubborn and headstrong. While, as in any relationship, there are times of disagreeement, there is much respect between the two signs and they are usually able to ride out any differences that may occur. Also they each possess a strong, enterprising and indomitable spirit and if some of their plans do not work out, they learn from experience and start on some new plan or project. The Tiger and Horse inspire, motivate and encourage each other and with a Tiger–Horse couple there are thrills and excitement as well as a few disappointments. One thing is certain – their life together is certainly never dull.

The Tiger and Horse also make dutiful and conscientious parents and, while they may be strict – woe betide any child who disobeys a Tiger or Horse parent – they care deeply for any children they have and make sure they want for nothing.

The Tiger and Horse are well suited and in love and marriage they can find much happiness. An excellent match.

TIGER AND GOAT

General Relations

The Tiger and Goat get on well together and can become firm friends. The Goat admires the enterprise, vitality and confidence of the Tiger, while the Tiger enjoys the Goat's easygoing and sociable manner. They relate well to each other, enjoy each other's company and together lead an active social life. General relations between these two signs are often good.

The Tiger and Goat can also work well together, particularly if their work is of a creative nature and allows each to generate ideas and make the most of their creative talents. The Tiger invariably takes the lead in any venture and is a valuable source of inspiration for the Goat. These two signs need, however, to deal with the financial aspects of any concern carefully as both tend to be free in their spending. With care and good fortune the Tiger and Goat can form a fine working relationship and there is trust and a good rapport between them.

Relations may not be so easy in parent–child relationships between these two signs. The Goat child is generally easygoing, sweet natured and needs much love and affection. However, the Tiger parent is often a disciplinarian and, while he loves his children dearly, his firm attitude may deeply affect the sensitive Goat child. When the Goat is parent and the Tiger the child, the Tiger's lively, headstrong and sometimes obstinate nature may cause the Goat parent many vexations. In both combinations, relations between parent and child need to be handled with much care.

In Love and Marriage

There is considerable attraction between the Tiger and Goat and, in love and marriage, they can find happiness and contentment. The Tiger is passionate, the Goat amorous and the physical attraction between them is strong.

The Goat enjoys the lively and enterprising nature of the Tiger. The Tiger is fun to be with, is most attentive and the Goat particularly values his sincere and honourable ways. The Goat is also reassured by the Tiger's strong and confident presence.

The Tiger, too, delights in the Goat's genial and sociable nature. The Goat is affectionate, tender and caring and is extremely supportive to the Tiger.

They are both great socializers, enjoy entertaining and between them have a wide circle of friends. Both also have creative and imaginative natures and they are never at a loss for projects to do, especially around the house.

However, for the Tiger and Goat to maintain their love and closeness each needs to show some willingness to adapt to the other. The Tiger can be frank and forthright in his views and without care may upset the more sensitive Goat, plunging the

Goat into one of his more pessimistic and despairing moods. Similarly, the Goat needs to allow the Tiger time to pursue his own interests rather than insist on complete togetherness in everything they do. The Tiger values his independence and freedom of movement. Another potential difficulty is that both signs tend to be spenders rather than savers and they need to keep a watchful eye over their finances.

Provided the Tiger and Goat are prepared to adapt to each other they can look forward to a contented life together. Each loves, supports and encourages the other dearly and each learns from their partner. The Goat may become more confident in outlook and the Tiger more diplomatic and refined. In love and marriage the Tiger and Goat can make a good match.

TIGER AND MONKEY

General Relations

The Tiger and Monkey are two lively, forceful and outgoing signs. Although they can get on well together, each is still slightly wary of the other. The honourable Tiger is distrustful of the Monkey's sometimes cunning and devious nature, while the Monkey resists the Tiger's domineering attitude. In terms of casual friendship and for socializing, these two signs can enjoy each other's company, but problems could emerge if their friendship goes any deeper.

When the Tiger and Monkey work together their different personalities may cause problems. Although they are both ambitious and enterprising, the Tiger cannot abide some of the Monkey's more devious notions, while the Monkey does not tolerate the Tiger's authoritarian stance. Each is wary of the other and, unless they are united in pursuit of a particular goal, they are likely to drift apart, each preferring to set about their work in their own individual way.

The Tiger and Monkey fare much better, however, in parent–child relationships. Both signs have a lively and adventurous disposition and while Tiger and Monkey children can sometimes be a little too spirited and need discipline and firm guidance, they nevertheless have a good rapport with their Tiger or Monkey parent. The parent nurtures the child's enthusiasm and keenness to learn and sets an example for the child to follow. Both Tiger and Monkey children admire the resourcefulness of a Tiger or Monkey parent and there is much love between them. In both combinations relations between parent and child are good.

In Love and Marriage

When the Tiger and Monkey first fall in love, there is passion, fun, excitement and lots of optimism and hope for the future. Both are lively and positive signs and for a time they only see the finer sides of each other's nature. However, their hopes may soon turn sour and, unless both are prepared to adapt, the long-term prospects for any union may be difficult.

Both signs are forceful, determined and like to have things their own way. The Tiger is honest and open in his feelings, while the Monkey can sometimes be evasive and such an attitude may prove intensely irritating to the Tiger. Nor does the Tiger care much for the Monkey's crafty and cunning ways. Similarly, the Monkey, who likes to keep tabs on everything, is suspicious of the Tiger's desire for a certain freedom in his actions and the Tiger may come to resent the Monkey's inquisitive and sometimes interfering nature. In times of disagreement both signs can be notoriously stubborn and neither readily gives ground to the other. The Tiger and Monkey can also be very competitive and this 'power struggle' for dominance, together with a mistrust of each other's motives, may undermine their relationship.

If the Tiger and Monkey can accept each other for what they are, show a willingness to adapt to each other and compromise in times of difficulties, then they may lead an active and contented life together. Both are enterprising, have a wide range of interests and are keen socializers.

However, a Tiger–Monkey match is not easy. They are two restless and domineering signs and their spirited natures often clash. In love and marriage this is a challenging and difficult match.

Tiger and Rooster

General Relations

The Tiger and Rooster have several traits in common; both like socializing and have lively and outgoing natures. But they both can be forceful and self-willed and each wants to dominate the other. They can also be candid and forthright, and when such frankness overflows – as it surely will – into criticism, then any slight accord that might have existed quickly degenerates. These signs may respect each other, but relations may not always be easy.

In business each sign may gain much from the other. The Tiger benefits from the Rooster's more methodical and consistent manner, while the Rooster gains from the Tiger's innovative ideas and enterprise. Their individual strengths may complement each other admirably, but first they need to settle their differences. Both the Tiger and Rooster can be competitive and each wants to take the lead. As both are also forthright and stubborn, difficulties may quickly emerge. If both signs are prepared to pool their strengths for a common objective, then they may make an effective partnership. But, more times than not, their conflicting natures come to the fore and undermine their efforts.

In parent–child relationships between these signs, there is love and affection but not always harmony. When the Rooster is parent and the Tiger the child, the firm Rooster parent can expect many battles with the self-willed and sometimes rebellious Tiger child. Admittedly the Rooster parent guides and educates the Tiger child well and encourages the child's diverse talents, but the Rooster finds it hard to accept the child's independent streak and desire to stray from the fold. Similarly, when the Tiger is parent and the Rooster the child, the Rooster child feels uneasy with the Tiger parent's impulsive and impetuous nature. The Rooster child seeks order, stability and routine and this is something which is not always found in a Tiger household. In both cases it is likely that the child opts to leave home early.

In Love and Marriage

Initially there may be a strong attraction between the Tiger and Rooster, both physical and mental. Each admires the strength and confidence of the other and both are also keen socializers. However, despite the strength of their feelings for each other, the longer-term prospects for their relationship may prove difficult.

Both the Tiger and Rooster are self-willed, like to have their own way and can be very forthright in expressing their views. In time – and it is likely to be sooner rather than later – their personalities and opinions clash and it is then that they see the wide differences that exist between them and that they need to reconcile if they are to remain together.

The Rooster is a great organizer, is methodical and meticulous. To the less disciplined Tiger, the Rooster at times appears fussy and pedantic; should, as is likely, the Tiger vent his feelings, strong words and harsh truths are exchanged. The Rooster does not take criticism lightly and, unlike some, the Tiger is strong enough to criticize the Rooster.

Similarly, the Tiger's impulsive nature disturbs the Rooster's sense of routine and the Rooster feels ill at ease with the Tiger's desire for a certain freedom and independence in his actions. The Rooster likes to keep tabs on everything around him and this is just not possible with a Tiger about.

With their forceful personalities, each will try to dominate the relationship and, unless there is a clear division of responsibilities, disagreements between them are bound to arise. Both are also ambitious and there may be a degree of competitiveness between them.

Basically, due to their frank, determined and stubborn natures, a match between a Tiger and Rooster is far from easy. The one hope is if they are prepared to accept the other for what they are, accept their different personalities and allow each other enough freedom to pursue their individual interests. If they can do this, it is possible relations between them may be satisfactory. But generally, in love and marriage, their relationship may be fraught with difficulties.

TIGER AND DOG

General Relations

The Tiger and Dog get on well together and can become firm friends. There is much trust and understanding between them and each benefits from the other's strengths. The Dog admires the enthusiasm, enterprise and courage of the Tiger but is a steadying influence on the Tiger's restless nature. The Tiger in turn values the Dog's loyal and dependable nature and does much to dispel the Dog's worrying and pessimistic tendencies. They enjoy each other's company and have many interests they can share. General relations between these two signs are invariably good.

The Tiger and Dog also work well together, either as colleagues or business partners. They trust and respect each other and can form a successful team. Each gains from the skills and strengths of the other. The Dog feels inspired and motivated by the enthusiasm of the Tiger, while the Tiger is mindful of the Dog's often cautionary but wise advice. The Tiger and Dog are loyal to each other and by combining their different skills and qualities they can enjoy considerable success.

In the parent–child relationship the Dog child gains much from the optimism and vitality of the Tiger parent and the Tiger parent does much to boost the confidence of a sometimes anxious Dog child. When the Dog is parent and the Tiger the child, the Tiger child thrives under the Dog parent's firm but caring guidance. The Dog parent guides the Tiger child well but at the same time gives the Tiger child the discipline and restraint that such a lively and restless child sometimes needs. In parent–child relationships between these two signs, there is much love, affection and respect.

In Love and Marriage

Although there are many personality differences between the Tiger and Dog, they complement each other extremely well. In love and marriage they can find much happiness and are ideally suited.

Both the Tiger and the Dog are loyal, trusting and honourable and each values these qualities in the other. There is an excellent rapport and understanding between them and each also gains from the strengths of the other. The sometimes pessimistic Dog can find reassurance and support from the more confident Tiger and gain from the Tiger's enterprising, lively and sociable nature. The Dog, too, admires the courage, willpower and altruism of the Tiger. The Tiger inspires the Dog and the Dog in turn is loyal, supportive and loving. In addition to the Dog's affection, the Tiger too will value the Dog's discretion, dependability and his advice. The Dog can be a steadying influence on his restless nature.

Each does much to help the other and as a couple they quickly become devoted to each other. They also both possess a caring and humanitarian nature and may be united in helping those less fortunate than themselves or championing some cause.

If the Tiger and Dog have a family they make admirable parents and, with the Tiger's adventurous spirit and the Dog's caring nature, they are a delight for any children that they have.

In love and marriage the Tiger and Dog make an excellent match. They are close, loving and supportive and each gains much from their relationship.

TIGER AND PIG

General Relations

Lively, sociable and with many interests in common, the Tiger and Pig get on well together. The Tiger enjoys the Pig's good-natured company as well as valuing the Pig's trust, sincerity and integrity. Similarly, the Pig delights in the Tiger's honest and open manner as well as appreciating the Tiger's energy, vivacity and enterprising nature. These two signs understand each other well and can become firm friends.

The Tiger and Pig are better suited on a social rather than business level, but when they work together they can still benefit from each other's strengths. The Pig gains from the Tiger's enthusiastic and innovative nature, while the Tiger values the Pig's commercial acumen. Both are ambitious and both work hard although the Tiger's impulsive, impatient and generous nature may be of concern to the more patient and financially astute Pig. However, as colleagues or business partners, they trust and respect each other and when they are committed to a specific objective their combined strengths can often lead them to success.

In the parent–child relationship the jovial and good-natured Pig child learns much from the enterprising Tiger parent and is likely to become more confident and outgoing as a result. However, there may be times when the Pig child would prefer a more peaceful and settled existence to the constant bustle that so often exists in a Tiger household. When the Pig is parent and the Tiger the child, the Tiger child values the love and affection of a kindly Pig parent, but it is in everyone's interests for the Pig parent to keep a firm rein on the ebullient Tiger child. Although the Pig parent may not be a strong disciplinarian, the Tiger child does need to be guided well if he is to make the most of his many abilities.

In Love and Marriage

The Tiger and Pig are often attracted to each other and make a splendid match. Both are passionate and sensual signs and there is a strong physical attraction between them. They understand each other well and are loyal and devoted to each other.

Both these signs are open and honest in their views and have a mutual dislike of hypocrisy and falsehood. They trust each other implicitly and there is an excellent rapport between them.

Together they have many interests they can share. Both are keen socializers and between them they have many friends. They also take much pleasure in entertaining and a party hosted by a Tiger–Pig couple is likely to be a truly splendid and unforgettable event. They also devote much energy to their home and family and the Pig, who understands the Tiger so well, does not begrudge the Tiger the certain degree of liberty he needs to pursue his own activities.

The Tiger and Pig also benefit from each other's qualities. The more patient and easygoing Pig is a stabilizing influence on the sometimes restless Tiger as well as being a useful curb on some of the Tiger's more impulsive and reckless notions. The Tiger greatly benefits from the Pig's wise and shrewd counsel, as well as from the Pig's financial judgement. The Tiger, in turn, is of great help to the Pig. The Pig, who is not as competitive as some, feels inspired and motivated by the zest and enthusiasm of the Tiger and the Tiger helps and encourages the Pig to realize his true potential. Also the Pig, with his deep faith in human nature, can sometimes be naive and vulnerable and the Tiger provides both protection and support for the Pig.

In love and marriage the Tiger and Pig have much to offer each other and together they can find happiness and contentment. They make a splendid couple and are well suited.

RABBIT AND RABBIT

General Relations

The Rabbit is one of the most companionable signs in the Chinese zodiac and two Rabbits can get on extremely well together. They have similar interests, particularly a love of conversation, and share an appreciation of the finer things in life. There is trust and understanding between them and a noticeable absence of discord – Rabbits go to great lengths to avoid unpleasantness and arguments. They enjoy each other's company and can become firm friends.

Rabbits are careful and shrewd workers and when they work together, either as colleagues or business partners, they make an effective combination. They both possess fine judgement, good financial skills and commercial acumen and there is a good level of trust and understanding between them. Neither is given to taking risks and through careful planning, good timing and determination, two Rabbits can do well. Their enterprise may not be the most dynamic, but it is certainly well run and founded on solid principles.

In the parent–child relationship there is much love between a Rabbit parent and Rabbit child. They understand each other well and have similar tastes and interests. The Rabbit parent takes much delight in guiding, teaching and assisting the Rabbit child, but at the same time is appreciative of many of the concerns of a young Rabbit; particularly the Rabbit child's sensitivity. The Rabbit parent does much to help and support the child and there is a close and enduring bond between them.

In Love and Marriage

With their romantic and passionate natures Rabbits are often attracted to each other and, in love and marriage, they make a good match. They share similar interests and outlooks and there is a close affinity between them. Both strive to establish a stable, secure and harmonious relationship and equally both go to great lengths to avoid arguments and unpleasantness.

Two Rabbits feel very much at ease with one another. They both enjoy conversation, sometimes even gossip, and may share an interest in the arts and the countryside as well as being keen socializers. They also both devote much time, energy and expense in creating and maintaining their home. With their usual fine taste, they make sure it is pleasingly furnished as well as being comfortable and cosy. Rabbits place much importance on their home and often stay in the same place for a long time.

A Rabbit couple do much to support each other. Both are conscientious and careful workers and, with their financial skills and good judgement, are often financially secure and able to enjoy a good standard of living. Both also take much pleasure in entertaining their friends and, with their genial natures, make superb hosts.

Provided a Rabbit couple do not face too many events which disturb their equilibrium and peaceful existence – Rabbits do not cope well in times of stress – they are truly content together. With their many mutual interests and similar outlooks they are well matched and, in love and marriage, make a fine, elegant and loving couple.

RABBIT AND DRAGON

General Relations

The Rabbit and Dragon can get on reasonably well together and, while their interests may not always coincide, they respect and like each other. The Rabbit appreciates the openness, sincerity and integrity of the Dragon, while the Dragon values the finesse and quiet, discreet manner of the Rabbit. Although the Dragon may enjoy a more energetic lifestyle to the Rabbit, these two signs can become trusted friends and confidantes.

The Rabbit and Dragon also work well together and their collective talents can make a successful combination. The Dragon's enthusiasm and drive will be of great benefit to the more cautious Rabbit, while the Rabbit's diplomacy, commercial acumen and more methodical nature helps the Dragon. Provided each is aware of their individual roles and remain committed to a specific objective, they can make a good and productive team.

In the parent–child relationship the Rabbit parent delights in the Dragon child's innovative ideas, his enthusiasm and keenness to learn, although the Dragon child's resolute and independent-minded ways could cause the Rabbit parent some anxiety. The Rabbit parent will, however, be justifiably proud of the Dragon child. When the Dragon is parent and the Rabbit the child, the Dragon parent does much to encourage the quiet and well-behaved Rabbit child and the child learns much from having such a caring and enterprising parent. Admittedly the Dragon parent's forthright nature may sometimes upset the sensitive Rabbit child, but there is always much love and respect between them.

In Love and Marriage

With both signs being passionate, sensuous and alluring, the Rabbit and Dragon are certainly attracted to each other and the early stages of their romance are truly blissful. However, if they are to sustain the deep love they feel for each other, both need to reconcile their different personalities.

The Dragon is far more outgoing than the Rabbit and likes to lead an active life, while the Rabbit is more restrained and refined. The Rabbit prefers the quieter things in life and without care their different outlooks could cause differences between them – the Rabbit being content at home, while the Dragon immerses himself in a wide range of activities. If both signs accept that they do have different interests and allow each other some personal freedom – rather than insisting on complete togetherness – then the Rabbit and Dragon can find contentment.

They can also gain from their different qualities. The Dragon, who can be blunt and forthright, learns much from the more gracious and tactful Rabbit, while the Rabbit benefits from the Dragon's confident and outgoing nature. Each also appreciates the integrity and sincerity of the other as well as being mindful of each other's views and advice. They are also both astute and diligent workers and between them have considerable earning ability; most Rabbit–Dragon couples are financially secure and able to enjoy a comfortable lifestyle. They also enjoy conversation, as well as spending time with their numerous friends.

In many respects the Rabbit and Dragon complement each other well, but for the match to be successful they each have to make allowances for their different interests and temperaments. If they can do this then, in love and marriage, they can find considerable happiness.

RABBIT AND SNAKE

General Relations

The Rabbit and Snake have much in common and can get on well together. Both are quiet, thoughtful signs; they are good natured and have a liking for the finer things in life. They share many interests and, with their love of conversation, pass many a happy hour spent in deep and wide-ranging discussion. They respect and understand each other and can become firm friends. General relations between these two signs are invariably good.

There is also the potential for the Rabbit and Snake to form a good working relationship. Both are skilled in financial matters and have considerable commercial acumen. Between them they have ideas and skills, but they may lack drive. Both tend to be cautious and great deliberators. When the Rabbit and Snake are firing on all cylinders they are a formidable and successful team, but so often the cylinders are idling while the Rabbit and Snake spend time talking and planning rather than acting.

In the parent–child relationship there is much love and affection between these two signs. Both Rabbit and Snake children are quiet and generally compliant and respond well to the love and attentiveness of a Rabbit or Snake parent. The parent and child have similar temperaments and share many interests. In both combinations there is a good rapport between the parent and child.

In Love and Marriage

The Rabbit and Snake are often deeply attracted to each other and in love and marriage they can find much happiness. Both are gentle, reflective signs who thrive in an orderly, secure and stable environment. Neither is given to great dramatic outbursts or seeks a frenzied lifestyle and together they strive for a peaceful and orderly existence.

They also share many interests. Both may have a liking for the arts and literature and share an appreciation of the finer things in life. Together they take great delight in furnishing and equipping their home so that it is not only pleasing to the eye but also extremely comfortable. Both Rabbits and Snakes are creatures of comfort and they enjoy many a pleasant evening sitting in their perfectly created lair relaxing and enjoying each other's company.

They understand each other well and give each other support and expert advice. Both Rabbit and Snake are perceptive and intuitive (even psychically gifted) signs and do much to help and assist the other. They are also both astute when dealing with financial matters, and through careful planning and shrewd investments – and possibly purchasing antiques and other items of value for their home – they may become wealthy in later life.

The one difficulty that may arise stems from the Snake's possessiveness. The Snake demands loyalty, which the Rabbit gives, but he likes to keep a tight rein on his partner and at times this tight rein may become somewhat oppressive for the Rabbit. In addition to their many joint interests, the Rabbit also wishes to pursue some independent interests and, for both their sakes, the Snake must allow this.

Generally, however, the Rabbit and Snake are ideally suited. With their refined and cultured tastes and their placid temperaments, each feels secure and content. In love and marriage the Rabbit and Snake can find much happiness together. An excellent and successful match.

RABBIT AND HORSE

General Relations

The Rabbit and Horse have very different temperaments and this does not make for good relations. The Horse has an active and outgoing nature and likes to live life to the full. The Rabbit, however, is much calmer and more placid and feels ill at ease with the energetic, lively and assertive Horse. Admittedly both are eloquent and persuasive speakers and may enjoy time together in conversation, but generally there is a certain coolness and reserve between them and they rarely become close friends.

This lack of rapport is also evident when they work together. The Horse is an active and enterprising individual, while the Rabbit is cautious and more a planner than the Horse. The Rabbit considers the Horse rash and impulsive, while the Horse views the Rabbit as a restraining influence. Similarly, differences over finance could emerge; the Horse spends freely and is a greater risk-taker than the more prudent Rabbit. Unless they are both committed to a specific objective or goal, the Rabbit and Horse generally do not work well together.

In the parent–child relationship a lively, adventurous and rather independent-minded Horse child brings many vexations for the placid Rabbit parent and relations between them are far from easy. When the Horse is parent and the Rabbit the child, the Horse parent does much to encourage the Rabbit child with his interests and education but the Rabbit child may not always feel at ease with a restless and sometimes short-tempered Horse parent. In both cases relations between these signs need to be handled with care.

In Love and Marriage

Although relations between Rabbit and Horse may not always be the best, these two signs can still fall very much in love. For all their differences, they each possess qualities that the other admires. They both have a strong sense of integrity, are discreet and trusting and both have a fondness for conversation and dialogue. There is also a strong physical attraction – the amorous Horse and the sensuous Rabbit. Love, sex and passion are high on the agenda.

However, while the early stages of their romance promise so

much, the love and affection they feel for each other may be difficult to sustain. The Rabbit seeks a secure, tranquil and orderly
existence and may feel unsettled by the Horse's restless and
volatile nature. The Horse also has a temper which, although
often short lived, again unnerves the Rabbit. The Rabbit loathes
any form of unpleasantness and is quite upset by the Horse's
outbursts. The Horse, however, may feel resentful that the
Rabbit is not as willing to share in his many activities as he
would like. The Rabbit is much more of a homelover than the
Horse. In addition, their different attitudes towards money may
pose problems. The Rabbit is careful and prudent, while the
Horse tends to spend his money more freely.

If both partners are able to go some way towards reconciling
their many differences, then it is just possible they may find
some contentment. But their personalities and outlooks are often
so different that after the early heady days of romance the way
ahead may be pitted with difficulties. In love and marriage this
is a challenging and turbulent match.

RABBIT AND GOAT

General Relations

The Rabbit and Goat get on very well together and can become
firm friends. They share many interests and both have a liking
for the finer things in life. They relate well to each other and as
both possess quiet and placid natures, each feels secure and
contented in the company of the other. Rabbits and Goats like
and trust each other and general relations between them are
invariably good.

The trust that exists between the Rabbit and the Goat also
helps them when they work together. To do well the Goat often

needs a motivating force behind him and the Rabbit provides this. Calm, methodical and financially astute, the Rabbit is an inspiration for the Goat and the Goat gives of his best, providing support, creativity and innovation. With discipline and a specific objective the Rabbit and Goat can prove a successful combination, especially if their work is of a creative or artistic nature.

In a parent–child relationship relations between these two signs are again good. The Rabbit or Goat child feels secure and happy in the peaceful and attentive atmosphere of a Rabbit or Goat household, and is given sufficient freedom and encouragement to develop and learn. Both parent and child often share similar interests – particularly a fondness for the arts and more creative pursuits – and the child flourishes under the parent's guidance. In both cases, irrespective of which sign is parent and which child, there is much love and understanding between them.

In Love and Marriage

The attraction between the Rabbit and Goat is strong and in love and marriage they can be blissfully happy. They are well suited and their many mutual interests and similar outlooks make them highly compatible. Both are genial, peaceloving signs; neither likes friction or living in a frenzied atmosphere and, as far as possible, they strive to make their lives secure, stable and comfortable. Indeed, both the Rabbit and Goat are creatures of comfort and with their strong artistic leanings their home is lovingly and tastefully furnished. They both appreciate the finer things in life and they strive to maintain a high standard of living.

There is a good understanding and rapport between the Rabbit and Goat and they offer each other love – much love – affection, loyalty and support. Both signs thrive in a secure and loving atmosphere and their relationship often brings out the best in the other. This is particularly so for the Goat, who needs an inspirational and supportive figure to help him realize his potential. The main danger to their relationship is if some calamity should strike. Neither copes well under stress and a crisis may easily undermine the stable and harmonious existence they have built up. However, as far as possible, these two signs do their utmost to avoid anything which would jeopardize their stable and secure existence and, more often than not, go through life enjoying themselves, savouring the fruits of their labours and loving and supporting each other. Their many joint interests and generally calm temperaments make them an ideal couple and in love and marriage they find much happiness. An excellent match.

RABBIT AND MONKEY

General Relations

For all their many differences, the Rabbit and Monkey get on well and can become good friends. The Monkey is quick to appreciate the Rabbit's good sense, quiet confidence and companionable nature, while the Rabbit enjoys the Monkey's zest, sparkle and resourcefulness. Both have wide interests, keen intellects and, with their mutual love of conversation, spend many enjoyable times in each other's company. They learn much from each other and both value their friendship.

When the Rabbit and Monkey work together, either as colleagues or business partners, relations between them may not be so favourable. The Rabbit is honest and ethical in his business dealings and is greatly concerned by the Monkey's sometimes dubious and crafty ploys. Nor is the Rabbit prepared to share in the risks that the enterprising Monkey wants to take and the

Monkey may find the Rabbit a restraining and inhibiting influence. In a business relationship there could well be misunderstanding and mistrust between them.

In the parent–child relationship the Rabbit parent may find the lively and adventurous Monkey child a disruptive influence on his calm and orderly existence. However, there is a great love between them and this grows as the Monkey child matures. Both have interests they can share and develop. When the Monkey is parent and the Rabbit the child, the Monkey parent loves the well-mannered and dutiful Rabbit child dearly. The child may not always be as outgoing as the Monkey parent may like, but the Monkey takes much delight in encouraging the Rabbit child's many interests. There is a good rapport between them.

In Love and Marriage

While the Rabbit and Monkey may have very distinct personalities, these two signs complement each other well. In love and marriage they can make a loyal, happy and contented pair.

The Monkey is the more outgoing of the two signs and the Rabbit delights in the Monkey's wit, confident and self-assured nature. Admittedly the Rabbit may not like some of the uncertainty and unpredictability that goes with a highly spirited Monkey, or, indeed, some of the Monkey's more crafty notions, but the Rabbit does value and appreciate the Monkey's skills. Similarly, the Monkey regards the Rabbit as a wise, loving and loyal partner. The Rabbit provides stability and order for the Monkey and the Monkey appreciates this. In their different ways, they help and support each other and there is good understanding between them.

Both the Rabbit and Monkey enjoy conversation and together have much fun talking about the many topics that interest them. They also cultivate joint interests and lead an active social life. Both are sociable signs, enjoy entertaining and between them have many friends.

The one factor which could disturb their relationship is the Rabbit's inability to cope with the Monkey's restlessness. The Monkey likes to keep himself busy and active and at times this may prove trying for the Rabbit, who craves for a more tranquil and peaceful existence. However, both signs mean much to each other and both do much to overcome any difficulties that occur in order to preserve their close relationship. In love and marriage the Rabbit and Monkey can make a good match, and one that often lasts.

RABBIT AND ROOSTER

General Relations

Relations between these two signs are poor. Their different personalities just do not gel and neither feels at ease in the company of the other. The Rooster is much too forthright and candid for the Rabbit's liking – the Rabbit can be sensitive and loathes criticism – while the Rooster finds the Rabbit reserved and withdrawn. Any friendship that develops between them is difficult to sustain.

When the Rabbit and Rooster are colleagues or business partners again relations may prove difficult. Although both are methodical, work hard and are honourable in their dealings, their different personalities bring them into conflict. The Rabbit just does not tolerate the bossiness, fussiness or domineering attitude of the Rooster, while the Rooster does not care much for the Rabbit's quiet, patient and more cautious manner. The Rooster likes hustle and bustle and activity and that is just not the way of the Rabbit.

In the parent–child relationship relations between these two signs need to be handled with great care. The Rabbit child values the attentiveness of the Rooster parent, but at the same time withers under the Rooster's sharp tongue. The Rooster speaks his mind and this, for the sensitive Rabbit child, can at times prove devastating. When the Rabbit is parent and Rooster the child, the Rabbit parent is pleased with the diligence and conscientiousness of the Rooster child, but may find it difficult to cope with the child's independent and sometimes headstrong attitude.

In Love and Marriage

This is a challenging match – the introverted Rabbit and the extroverted Rooster. Although each may recognize the other's qualities, their different personalities may present them with many difficulties. In love and marriage this is not an easy relationship.

The Rabbit is quiet, refined and tactful, while the Rooster can be brash, flamboyant and candid. Many times the sensitive Rabbit is unnerved or feels uncomfortable at the Rooster's utterances. If a Rabbit–Rooster relationship stands any chance of surviving, the Rooster needs to be much more diplomatic and more aware of the Rabbit's feelings.

Another potential difficulty is that the Rabbit craves for a quiet and peaceful existence, while the Rooster likes to lead a more active and energetic lifestyle. The Rabbit also does not care for all the Rooster's bluster and swagger, while the Rooster finds the Rabbit withdrawn and at times pedantic. Each has difficulty in adjusting to the other.

In view of their different personalities it takes an exceptional couple to make this relationship work. However, if they can, each can gain from the other. The Rabbit may become more assertive and outgoing under the Rooster's influence, while the Rooster becomes more refined and relaxed in his attitude. Hopefully, too, the Rooster may become less candid.

It takes many adjustments on both sides for this relationship to work and generally, in love and marriage, the Rabbit and Rooster are not well suited. A difficult and challenging match.

Rabbit and Dog

General Relations

Rabbits and Dogs like each other and relations between them are good. They are both loyal and caring signs and often share similar interests and outlooks. There is much respect and understanding between them and they relate well to each other. The Rabbit and Dog often become close and lifelong friends.

Relations between these two signs are also satisfactory on a business level. Both are diligent and hard working. They are honourable in their business dealings and are prepared to pool their strengths for a common objective. When things are going well the Rabbit and Dog make a powerful team – it is only when they face problems or a downturn in activity that the difficulties emerge. The Dog is prone to bouts of anxiety and the Rabbit does not cope well under stress; difficult situations may put serious strains on an otherwise excellent working relationship.

In the parent–child relationship relations are again good. The quiet and generally obedient Rabbit child does much to please the dutiful Dog parent and there is a strong bond between them. Similarly, when the Rabbit is parent and the Dog the child, the Dog child looks to his parent for love, affection and security which the Rabbit parent is happy to give. Admittedly the Rabbit parent may despair of the Dog child's sometimes moody or stubborn nature but, underneath it all, there is much love between them.

In Love and Marriage

The Rabbit and Dog have much in common and are often deeply attracted to each other. Both seek a stable and secure existence and there is a good level of trust between them. In love and marriage the Rabbit and Dog are well suited.

Both attach much importance to their home and, with the Rabbit's fine artistic taste and Dog's practical skills, their home is a pride to both. In addition to their home, they have many interests they can share and both also take much pleasure in entertaining their friends. The Rabbit and Dog seem to come into their own at small social gatherings.

They also appreciate each other's qualities. The Rabbit delights in the loyalty, dependability and sincerity of the Dog, while the Dog values the refined and companionable ways of the Rabbit. They also do much to help each other. Although both may appear outwardly confident each can, however, be prone to periods of self-doubt. The Dog tends to be a worrier and sometimes a pessimist, while the Rabbit does not cope well under stress or when subjected to sudden change. Each is a useful prop for the other and together they give each other valuable support, reassurance and advice.

Both Rabbits and Dogs also take considerable pride in their appearance and together can make a striking and good-looking couple. With their rapport, similar outlooks and the strong physical attraction they have for each other, the Rabbit and Dog are well suited. Their love, loyalty and devotion for each other is unquestioned and together these two signs can find much happiness and contentment.

RABBIT AND PIG

General Relations

Both Rabbits and Pigs are highly sociable signs and can get on well together. They often share similar interests and there is a good rapport between them. They respect and understand each other well and, while the Pig may not always be as refined as the Rabbit may wish, general relations between these two signs are invariably good.

The Chinese consider that Pigs are lucky in business and money matters and this, combined with the Rabbit's shrewd sense, makes a working relationship between these two signs highly favourable. Both work hard and their persistence and determination helps them in any venture. Each also gains from the other. The Rabbit feels reassured by having such an honourable, robust and resilient partner, while the Pig values the Rabbit's organizational abilities and perceptive advice. There is much trust and respect between them and, as colleagues or business partners, they can enjoy much success.

In the parent–child relationship, no matter whether it is Rabbit parent and Pig child or vice versa, there is always a close under-standing between these signs. Both Rabbit and Pig children are caring and dutiful and appreciate the security, stability and comfort found in a Rabbit or Pig home. Parent and child share many interests and there is much love and respect between them. As in all Rabbit–Pig relationships, these are two signs that get on well together.

In Love and Marriage

The Rabbit and Pig are highly compatible and in love and marriage they can find much happiness. Both are genial and sociable signs and have a good understanding of each other.

They share many interests – particularly a love of the country-side and nature – as well as enjoying an active social life. They are also both peaceloving signs and go to great lengths to avoid arguments and disputes. Both Rabbits and Pigs value harmony and a stable and stress-free lifestyle.

Both are also passionate and sensual signs and there is a strong physical attraction between them. They love and cherish each other dearly and there is much loyalty between them.

The Rabbit and Pig couple also work well together as a team, endeavouring to make their home stylish and comfortable, for both are very much creatures of comfort. Both are also diligent in their work and with their skills and financial acumen they are often financially secure and able to maintain the high standard of living they so much enjoy.

The Rabbit and Pig are also respectful of each other's feelings. The Pig is far more resilient than the Rabbit and the Pig makes every effort to shoulder many of the burdens that can so vex the Rabbit. Similarly, the Rabbit acts as a trusted adviser for the Pig, giving advice that the Pig, sometimes gullible and naive, greatly benefits from.

In love and marriage there is harmony, contentment and respect between these two signs. They are well suited and, with their shared interests and desire for a comfortable and harmonious existence, they make an ideal match. Together they share much good fortune.

DRAGON AND DRAGON

General Relations

Dragons are lively and sociable signs and for a time two Dragons can get on well together. They enjoy each other's company, have a lively exchange of views and share in much fun. However, Dragons can also be domineering and forthright and, in time, their views, interests and opinions may well clash. For the short to medium term general relations between two Dragons are good; after that difficulties between them may emerge.

Dragons are enterprising and diligent workers and when two Dragons work together, either as colleagues or business partners, they can make a formidable team. They both set high standards and are enthusiastic, determined and ambitious. When they are committed to a particular objective, their combined strengths – together with their luck – help them to success. However, both are assertive and domineering characters and they would do well to agree upon a division of responsibilities. If not, they may end up vying with each other for control and thereby undermining what may be a successful working partnership.

As a parent, the Dragon is strict and fair minded. Children know where they stand with a Dragon parent and when the child is also a Dragon the relationship between parent and child is strong. There is a considerable empathy between them and the Dragon parent does much to support and encourage his lively and enthusiastic child. Admittedly there are times when the strong and sometimes independent-minded child clashes with an equally strong-minded parent, but generally they understand each other well and there is much love between them. A Dragon child gains much from a Dragon parent.

In Love and Marriage

Dragons are often attracted to each other. Vibrant, attractive and full of life, Dragons make marvellous companions. Two Dragons in love can be passionately happy – they have fun and excitement and together will talk of great plans, of hopes and of the opportunities that await them. Their love and devotion to each other is total. Both are optimists and both like to live life to the full.

However, while the early stages of their relationship has so much to offer they need to proceed carefully if they are to maintain such a happy and harmonious state. Both can be stubborn and forthright and, with their forceful and domineering natures, each strives to get their own way. However, though there may be times of discord, there is also much love and respect between them and they will learn to reconcile their differences. Each also allows the other a certain independence rather than insists on complete togetherness in everything they do. It is also in their interests if they have a clear division of responsibilities in their home life and try not to interfere too much in each other's duties.

Both partners are hard and enterprising workers and between them have considerable earning abilities. Together they are materially well off and able to indulge in their wide range of interests. They may also both share a love of outdoor activities and be keen travellers as well as leading an active social life.

If they can come to terms with their dominant and strong-willed natures then, in love and marriage, two Dragons can make a dynamic, outgoing and striking couple and their life together is rich and fulfilling. With care, this can be a good match but so much depends on the partners being able to reconcile their strong-willed personalities.

DRAGON AND SNAKE

General Relations

Relations between the Dragon and Snake are excellent. Although they have different personalities, the Dragon being far more outgoing than the quiet and thoughtful Snake, these signs just gel. They understand and trust each other and there is great respect between them. The Dragon values the Snake's wisdom and perceptiveness, while the Snake is intoxicated by the charm, zest and dynamism of the Dragon. The Dragon and Snake genuinely like and admire each other and can become lifelong friends.

A business relationship between these two signs can also be successful, with each sign benefiting from the strengths and skills of the other. The Snake is shrewd, calculating and plans his activities with the utmost care and is a useful check on some of the Dragon's more rash and impulsive notions. The Dragon gains much from having a wily Snake as a business partner. Similarly, the vigour and enthusiasm with which the Dragon conducts his activities is an important stimulus for the Snake. In business, the Dragon and Snake are well suited and can enjoy great success.

There is also a good rapport and understanding between these two signs in a parent–child relationship. The Snake parent takes much delight in sharing his ideas, knowledge and general outlook on life (Snakes are great philosophers) with a receptive Dragon child. The Dragon child responds well to the attentiveness of the quiet and caring Snake parent. When the Dragon is parent and the Snake the child, the compliant Snake child values the firm but fair rule of the Dragon parent and there is again a great bond between them. In both cases, irrespective of the combination, there is a lasting love and loyalty between parent and child.

In Love and Marriage

The Dragon and Snake make an excellent match and in love and marriage can find much happiness.

There is a strong attraction between these signs, both physical and mental. The calm, alluring and seductive charms of the Snake prove irresistible to the Dragon, while the Snake is attracted by the warmth, vitality and sincerity of the Dragon. In their different ways each complements the other. There is trust and understanding between them and the physical attraction is strong. Both signs have a large sexual appetite and neither is disappointed.

Each sign also benefits from the relationship. The Snake becomes more outgoing and sociable, with the energy and enthusiasm of the Dragon being a useful boost for the serpent. The Dragon, in turn, gains from the Snake's wise counsel and cautious nature. The Snake is a useful curb on the Dragon's sometimes impatient and impulsive manner. Together they help and support each other and as both are usually adept in financial matters, between them they can accumulate great wealth.

The one problem that may emerge in this relationship stems from the Snake's possessiveness. If the Dragon should ever give the Snake grounds for jealously, or finds the Snake's possessiveness too great, difficulties may arise. But generally, these two signs respect each other so much that such a problem is a rare occurrence.

In love and marriage these two make a marvellous couple. There is a great rapport and understanding between them and they are ideally suited.

DRAGON AND HORSE

General Relations

There is a liking and respect between these two signs and for a time general relations are good. Both are lively and adventurous characters and there is trust and understanding between them. They often share many interests and quite happily join forces for activities they wish to undertake. For the short to medium term the Dragon and Horse can become close and almost inseparable friends, but each sign possesses an independent streak and, unless there is a romantic involvement, over time they may well decide to go their separate ways in search of new friends and adventures.

In a working situation there is a good level of trust and respect between the Horse and Dragon. Both are diligent and hard workers and, when committed to a specific goal, their enthusiasm, energy and vigour leads them to considerable success. They also benefit from each other's strengths. The Dragon possesses a stronger imagination and vision than the Horse, while the Horse is more practical and realistic than the Dragon. By combining their skills they create a powerful force. However, both signs are ambitious and strong willed and in time new challenges, together with a desire to prove themselves on their own, may eventually pull them apart.

In the parent–child relationship, relations between these signs are good. The Horse parent delights in the versatility, intelligence and enterprising ways of a Dragon child and the Horse parent does much to encourage and support the child. When the Dragon is parent and the Horse the child, the Horse child values the lively and enterprising nature of a Dragon parent and strives to live up to his parent's expectations. In both cases there are many interests that the parent and child can share and there is much love and understanding between them.

155

In Love and Marriage

There is considerable attraction between the Dragon and Horse. Both are lively and outgoing signs. Both are attractive and presentable and, with their good looks and engaging personalities, each is drawn to the other. They are both passionate and amorous signs and the early stages of their romance are happy and blissful. They also find they have much in common, including a love of conversation, socializing, the outdoor life and travel. Both are blessed with much energy and they live and enjoy life to the full.

As a couple the Dragon and Horse can find much happiness, but problems may emerge between them. Both are forceful and domineering signs and, unless they can agree on a clear division of responsibilities in their home life, there may be many tussles between them. Both can be forthright in expressing their views and, with the Horse's temper and Dragon's frankness, life at times may become heated. Horses can also be self-centred and Dragons demanding, so sometimes their personalities and viewpoints clash. All these areas may undermine their relationship, but the Dragon and Horse mean much to each other and with goodwill and understanding they should be able to reconcile any differences that may occur. They will also benefit from each other's strengths. The Horse particularly values the enthusiasm, vigour and sincerity of the Dragon, while the Dragon admires the diligence, eloquence and practical nature of the Horse. Both are loyal and faithful and there is considerable trust between them. They also allow each other a certain independence to pursue their own interests and this is something both very much appreciate.

With their lively natures, the Dragon and Horse can lead an active and fulfilling life together and, providing they can reconcile any differences that occur, they can make a good match.

DRAGON AND GOAT

General Relations

The Dragon and Goat get on reasonably well together. The Goat delights in the Dragon's lively and confident manner, while the Dragon admires the Goat's sociable and creative nature. They relate well to each other and are likely to lead an active social life. For the short to medium term general relations between them are good. However, in time, the Dragon may begin to lose patience with the Goat's capricious and fickle ways and the Goat, always keen to make new friends, may forsake the Dragon for other company. Although these two signs can become friends, rarely is this a long-lasting friendship and with the Dragon and Goat it is more a case of enjoying their friendship while it lasts.

A Dragon and Goat can, for a time, work reasonably well together. The Dragon, who is far more assertive than the Goat, takes the lead in any enterprise and is a valuable source of inspiration and motivation for the Goat. The Dragon brings out the best in the Goat and the Goat values the bold, enterprising and honourable ways of the Dragon. The Dragon, in turn, appreciates the Goat's artistic and creative talents and both are capable of devising many original ideas. When they are united in pursuing a specific objective they can make a successful combination although, with the Dragon's restlessness and Goat's capriciousness, the durability of their working relationship may not be great.

In the parent–child relationship the lively and sometimes demanding Dragon child may prove a handful for the more placid Goat parent. However, despite the worry and tribulations that a Dragon child may bring, the Goat parent is truly proud of the abilities and resourcefulness of the Dragon child and there is much love between them. When the Dragon is parent and the

Goat the child, the Dragon parent's direct and forthright nature may sometimes prove unsettling for a sensitive Goat child. However, the Dragon makes a fine parent and is quick to spot where the Goat child's talents lie and does much to encourage and support the child. Although relations between the Dragon parent and Goat child may not always be easy, the Goat child benefits from having a firm but loving and attentive Dragon as parent.

In Love and Marriage

The attraction between the Dragon and Goat can be great and these two signs can fall very much in love. Both signs are highly sociable and have lively temperaments. The Dragon is very much taken by the Goat's elegance, charm and wit, while the Goat admires the Dragon's vivaciousness and strength of character. The Dragon is bold, outgoing and confident; all qualities that the Goat very much admires. There is also a strong physical attraction between them and their sex life is immensely satisfying for both.

Together the Dragon and Goat have much fun. The Dragon feels heartened by the Goat's devotion and reliance and the Goat is comforted and reassured by the Dragon. In love, each has much to offer the other and a romance between them is something neither ever forgets. Unfortunately, however, this happy state of affairs may not continue in marriage.

For all the Goat's many qualities, he can be temperamental and capricious and the Dragon may quickly tire of the Goat's fickle nature and swings of mood. Similarly, the Goat feels ill at ease with the Dragon's restless and somewhat independent nature, and also views some of the Dragon's more ambitious projects as a little too risky. The Goat seeks an easy and peaceful life with a strong measure of security, and this is not always possible with an active and impulsive Dragon about.

For a marriage between the Dragon and Goat to succeed, there needs to be much understanding on both sides and this may prove difficult. In time the Dragon may feel the Goat too much of a restrictive influence and the Goat may find the Dragon too volatile. From such a promising start, a marriage between the Dragon and Goat may fail to live up to expectations and prove a disappointment for both.

DRAGON AND MONKEY

General Relations

The Dragon and Monkey are two lively and sociable signs and they get on well together. They both enjoy each other's company and, with their many mutual interests and enthusiastic and energetic natures, they can become lifelong friends. There is trust and understanding between them and should either suffer a reversal in fortune – as, indeed, could be likely, as both are risk takers – the other is there to support, encourage and advise. There is a spirit of trust and camaraderie between them and general relations between these two signs are invariably excellent.

Their rapport also assists them when they work together, either as colleagues or business partners. Both signs are resourceful and set about their activities with zest and enthusiasm. The Monkey is adept at spotting opportunities and the Dragon is certainly not averse to taking risks. Admittedly their impetuous natures may sometimes lead them into difficulties, but the Monkey is an expert at extricating himself and others from problems and their skills, enterprise and sheer ability win them through. The Dragon and Monkey work well together and can enjoy great success. Each motivates and inspires the other.

In the parent–child relationship there is also a good bond

between these signs. Both Dragon and Monkey children are resourceful, quick to learn and have lively and spirited natures. In both cases the parent does much to encourage and support the Dragon or Monkey child, as well as enjoying the child's sociable and good-humoured nature. Irrespective of which sign is parent and which is child, the child learns much from the parent and there is a good rapport and understanding between them.

In Love and Marriage

The Dragon and Monkey are ideally suited to each other and in love and marriage they can establish a tender, caring and loving relationship. They mean much to each other and enjoy considerable happiness together.

Both signs are lively and outgoing and possess energy and enthusiasm. In addition to their many interests, they like to lead an active social life and between them have a large circle of friends.

The Dragon greatly admires the Monkey. The Monkey has wit, guile, zest and talent. The Monkey is a quick thinker and highly resourceful, all qualities that the Dragon appreciates. Similarly, the Monkey values the Dragon's bold and confident manner. The Dragon is sincere and trusting and, like the Monkey, is prepared to stand up for what he believes and go after what he wants. Both are doers, both action orientated and as a couple they work as a team, each helping the other with his various activities. Both pay great heed to the other's advice – the Dragon is constantly marvelling at the Monkey's resourcefulness and ability to sort out problems, while the Monkey places much reliance on the Dragon's opinions and views.

Both the Dragon and Monkey can be flamboyant in their gestures and mannerisms and, to some, they might appear a zany, eccentric or unconventional couple, but neither cares. Each loves and values the other and they combine their strengths, go forth and do what they want. If a Dragon and Monkey couple should decide to go into business together, they may enjoy considerable success. The Dragon and Monkey are well suited and find much happiness together. A good match.

Dragon and Rooster

General Relations

The Dragon and Rooster have much in common. They are lively and spirited signs, both with a mind of their own. There is respect and trust between them and they can become firm friends. They are keen socializers, are likely to share many interests and enjoy each other's company. Both like to make full use of their time and both are outgoing and enterprising. They understand each other well and general relations between them are invariably good.

The Dragon and Rooster can also form a useful working relationship, with each benefiting from skills of the other. The Rooster gains from the vision and enthusiasm of the Dragon, while the Dragon benefits from the organizational skills of the Rooster. The Rooster is also a useful curb on some of the Dragon's more reckless notions. They are both diligent and hard workers and there is much trust and loyalty between them. As colleagues and business partners, the Dragon and Rooster get on well and can make a successful team.

In the parent–child relationship relations between these two signs need to be handled with care. Both Dragon and Rooster parents can be strict and authoritarian and a Rooster parent does not take kindly to the strong and independent-minded ways of a Dragon child, while the Dragon parent sometimes loses patience with a demanding and sometimes fussy Rooster child. However, while the parent and child may clash from time to time, the parents still do much to encourage the abilities of their often gifted Dragon or Rooster child.

In Love and Marriage

The Dragon and Rooster make a good match and in love and marriage they find happiness together. They are both lively, outgoing and sociable signs and they have many interests in common. They relate well to each other and there is considerable respect and accord between them.

As a couple they are not only able to combine their different talents successfully but also benefit from each other's strengths. The more conservative Rooster is a stabilizing influence on the Dragon and provides method, order and planning to the Dragon's sometimes hectic lifestyle. Similarly the Dragon helps to break down some of the Rooster's reserve and makes the Rooster a little more relaxed and tolerant.

Between them they have many friends and both take much delight in partying and entertaining. They also allow each other time to maintain their own separate interests; something which is essential for both. There is freedom, respect and trust in their relationship and they understand each other well.

The main problem in their relationship is that both can be notoriously forthright in expressing their views. The Rooster is famed for being candid and the Dragon is certainly no diplomat, so they are likely to have many heated discussions and arguments. To compensate for this neither is left in any doubt as to where the other stands on any matter and, in any case, both much prefer straight, direct and honest talking.

With some of the other Chinese signs, the Dragon outshines and dominates his partner, but not so with the Rooster. The Dragon has met his match. Each plays an equal part in their relationship, each is mindful of the other. Admittedly, as in all relationships, there are good times and bad, but the Dragon and

Rooster are strong, resilient signs and together they weather the storms, helping and assisting each other all the way. In love and marriage both gain much from their relationship.

DRAGON AND DOG

General Relations

There is little accord between the Dragon and Dog and general relations between these two signs are poor. Their outlooks and personalities are often very different and neither has much time for the other. The Dog sees the Dragon as being brash and opinionated, while the Dragon has little patience for the serious and sometimes moralizing tones of the Dog. These signs find it hard to accept and understand the other and rarely become friends.

Their lack of rapport also hampers business relationships. Both find it hard to trust the other and there may well be a battle for supremacy. The bold and enterprising Dragon is constantly trying to impose his will and ideas on the Dog, and the Dog resists this. The Dog is critical of the Dragon's enterprising and sometimes risky notions, while the Dragon finds the Dog's cautionary approach too much of a restrictive influence. As colleagues and business partners, Dragons and Dogs are often pulling in opposite directions and are unlikely to work successfully together.

There are also difficulties between these two signs in a parent–child relationship. A Dragon parent may find it hard to understand the concerns and worries of a sometimes anxious Dog child, while a Dog parent views the lively, spirited and independent-minded ways of a Dragon child with some misgivings. In both cases much care and understanding is needed. These signs find it hard to get on well together and it is worth every effort on the parent's side to understand their child a little better. If not, the bond between them may never be strong.

In Love and Marriage

Tradition does not bode well for relations between the Dragon and Dog and, in love and marriage, there may be difficulties. Sometimes these can be overcome and the Dragon and Dog can find contentment, but this is more the exception than the rule.

The essential problem lies in their different personalities and outlooks on life. The Dragon is lively and outgoing, sometimes to the point of being flamboyant and, while this impresses some, it only annoys the Dog. The Dog sees things as they are. He is a direct, matter-of-fact and no-nonsense sort of person and he expects others to be the same. The Dragon's showiness does not wash with the Dog, and the Dog also finds it hard to trust or relate to such an impulsive and impetuous character. Similarly, the Dragon finds it hard to understand the personality of the Dog. Although loyal, caring and dutiful, the Dog can be a worrier and suffer from bouts of pessimism and anxiety. During these times the Dog needs attention, understanding and a sympathetic ear and this is something that the Dragon may not fully appreciate. Both the Dragon and Dog can also be forthright and stubborn and there may be a constant vying for dominance of the relationship.

Another area of difficulty is that both signs tend to have different interests. The Dog is often very involved in humanitarian matters and, on a social level, much prefers a quiet meal with friends to a lot of partying. The Dragon, on the other hand, has a welter of interests, likes to be very much at the centre of things (he is, with his extrovert personality, something of a showman) and enjoys an active social life. Their interests and views often clash. The one compensating factor is that the Dragon appreciates the loyalty of the Dog and the Dog may become more outgoing and self-assured under the influence of the Dragon. But, generally, in love and marriage, relations between the Dragon and Dog are poor. This is a difficult and challenging match.

DRAGON AND PIG

General Relations

The Dragon and Pig enjoy each other's company and general relations between them are good. Both are lively and sociable signs and they like to live life to the full. They both enjoy an active social life and are respectful of each other's views. They admire and trust each other, have many interests in common and can become firm friends.

As colleagues and business partners, the Dragon and Pig work well together and can form a successful working relationship. The Dragon is born under the sign of luck and the Pig is generally fortunate in financial matters; together they can do well. They trust each other and both attach much importance to honesty and openness in their business dealings. Each also benefits from the skills of the other. The Pig benefits from the Dragon's enterprise and enthusiasm, while the Dragon gains from the Pig's more persistent and patient manner. Both are hard working and keen to give of their best. In business, the Dragon and Pig can accomplish much together.

In the parent–child relationship the amiable Pig child learns much from the firm, but caring guidance of the Dragon parent. The Pig child always tries to live up to the Dragon parent's expectations and there is a good bond between them. When the Pig is parent and the Dragon the child, the Pig parent may not always understand the independent-minded ways of the Dragon child, but still loves and cherishes his lively and gifted child dearly. There is a strong affinity between them.

In Love and Marriage

There is a considerable attraction between these two signs and in love and marriage the Dragon and Pig can form a close and loving relationship.

The Dragon is very much taken with the Pig's jovial and easy-going nature and finds the Pig good and interesting company. They share many interests, are keen socializers and there is a strong physical attraction between them. Both the Dragon and Pig are passionate and sensual signs and their sex life is active and satisfying.

The Dragon also admires the trusting and honourable nature of the Pig and delights in the Pig's affection and support. The Pig is a most attentive and caring partner and this is something that the Dragon readily appreciates.

The Pig also gains much from a Dragon partner. The Pig, who is not as competitive as some, is inspired by the Dragon and imbued with a greater confidence and enthusiasm. The Dragon encourages the Pig and helps the Pig to make the most of his many talents. The Dragon also protects the sometimes gullible Pig. Together, in their different ways, they complement each other very well.

The Dragon and Pig are hard-working signs and between them have considerable earning abilities. Many Dragon–Pig couples are materially well off and are able to enjoy a good and comfortable standard of living. They put much energy into creating and maintaining their home and the Dragon, in particular, very much appreciates the Pig's superb homemaking talents.

Generally the Dragon and Pig go through life loving, encouraging and supporting each other. Both gain much from their relationship and in love and marriage the Dragon and Pig are well suited.

Snake and Snake

General Relations

On a purely social level the Snake enjoys the company of another Snake. They have many interests in common, including an appreciation of the arts and the finer things in life. Being such deep thinkers they delight in exchanging their views and their discussions are often profound and intellectually stimulating. Snakes find each other interesting and challenging company and general relations between them can, for a time, be good.

When two Snakes work together, either as colleagues or business partners, their relations are amiable and they may enjoy some measure of success, but generally this is not the best of combinations. Snakes are thoughtful creatures, given to periods of deliberation and reflection. Together they may create some wonderful and original ideas, but there may be long delays before they put their plans and ideas into action. To fulfil his potential the Snake really needs a colleague or partner who is more dynamic and action orientated than another meditative and cautious Snake.

In a parent–child relationship relations between the Snake parent and Snake child need careful handling. There is great affection between them, but there may not always be total accord. Although both are of the same sign, the Snake parent may experience difficulty in penetrating the Snake child's quiet and private world. The Snake child can also be a late developer and this may cause the Snake parent some anxiety. The Snake child often tests the patience of a Snake parent, but despite any problems that might arise there is always an enduring bond between them.

In Love and Marriage

Snakes can bewitch and mesmerize each other. With their strong seductive powers and their many mutual interests, Snakes can easily fall for one another and a love affair between two Snakes is intense, passionate and sexually very active.

As the Snake is a calm and placid sign, a Snake couple strives for a quiet, orderly and peaceful existence. They plan their activities carefully and, as far as possible, try to avoid a hectic or frenzied way of life. They also enjoy creating their home, particularly as both have exquisite and refined tastes. Both may be artistically inclined and may enjoy literature, music and the arts. They also both have enquiring minds and enjoy conversing about all manner of subjects.

For a time a Snake couple can be blissfully happy, content in their own private and secure world. However, there are serious problems that they need to address and which, if they are not careful, may undermine and even destroy their relationship.

The Snake is a possessive creature and each Snake keeps close tabs on the other. If either gives the other any cause for jealousy or resentment, there may be great problems between them. An embittered Snake can be very hard to live with and Snakes do not forgive or forget easily. Also, as Snakes are so exclusive, there is a danger that a Snake couple may keep themselves to themselves to such a degree they may become stale and bored. Ideally, if their relationship is to last, each must allow the other the opportunity to pursue his own individual interests rather than insist on complete togetherness.

It has been said that two Snakes cannot live under the same roof and even though there may be much attraction between them, their possessive natures are so strong that this may give rise to many problems between them. In love and marriage, from an often close and intense start, the long-term prospects for a match between two Snakes may prove challenging.

Snake and Horse

General Relations

The Snake and Horse find each other interesting company and relations between them are cordial, although not necessarily close. The Horse recognizes the Snake's sharp and incisive mind and values the Snake's opinions, while the Snake delights in the Horse's charming and eloquent manner. Both have many interests and it is likely that at least some of these will coincide and that there is some common ground between them. There is respect between these two signs, but the Horse has an adventurous and somewhat independent spirit and relations may cool as the Snake prefers to go his way rather than be drawn too closely into the Horse's busy and more active lifestyle.

As colleagues and business partners the Snake and Horse make a reasonably good combination, with each benefiting from the skills and strengths of the other. The Snake thinks and plans, while the Horse put the plans into action. The hard-working and enthusiastic Horse motivates the Snake and helps the Snake to become more action orientated. The Snake, in turn, provides the Horse with much useful advice and also prevents the Horse from acting rashly or hotheadedly, as the Horse can sometimes be prone to do. When they are united in securing a certain objective, a Snake–Horse partnership can prove an effective combination.

In a parent–child relationship relations between the Snake and Horse may prove tricky and need to be handled with care.

The Snake parent finds the Horse child independent and strong willed, and communication between them may at times be difficult. The Horse child may also view the Snake parent as being too possessive and protective and choose to leave home early. When the Horse is the parent and the Snake the child, again there may be problems. The quiet and reflective Snake child may feel ill at ease with the busy and active lifestyle that the Horse parent tends to lead. The Snake prefers order, routine and consistency and some of these may be lacking in a Horse household. Again, there may not be a good understanding between parent and child.

In Love and Marriage

The attraction between the Snake and Horse can be strong and their relations intense. The Horse falls for the seductive charms of the Snake, while the Snake delights in the passion and amour of the Horse. Together they can have much fun, lead an active social life and share some common interests. Both are likely to be widely read and enjoy intelligent conversation. The more outgoing Horse appreciates the quiet, calm and considerate manner of the Snake and the Snake values the faithfulness and loyalty of the Horse.

When the Snake and Horse fall in love both signs receive much from their relationship. However, over the longer term there may be problems ahead. Fortunately these are not insurmountable and there are many Snakes and Horses who are happily wed, but for this to be so each needs to develop a good understanding of the other.

The problems arise from their different personalities. The Snake can be possessive and the Horse, who enjoys a certain independence, may feel restricted by the Snake's attitude. It is in the Snake's interests to allow the Horse the time and freedom to continue his own interests as well as encouraging those that they can share. The Snake, who can be promiscuous, also needs to curb his sometimes flirtatious nature. The Horse is faithful and loyal and expects his partner to be the same.

The Horse is, however, much more lively and adventurous than the Snake and the Horse needs to recognize that the Snake cannot be hurried or hassled against his will. To live in harmony the Horse needs to develop a great deal of patience and, for one so active, the Snake's leisurely attitude can sometimes prove exasperating.

Providing both partners are prepared to go some way to adjusting to each other, their relations in love and marriage can be satisfying. The placid Snake can be a steadying influence on the sometimes volatile nature of the Horse and also does much to defuse the Horse's quick temper. The Horse, in turn makes the Snake more outgoing and adventurous, both of which are in the Snake's interests. With care and understanding both can gain from their relationship, but for the match to survive their often wonderful romance, each needs to show a willingness to adapt to the other. From a good start, this can often turn into a challenging match.

SNAKE AND GOAT

General Relations

The Snake and Goat are both calm and easygoing signs and general relations between them are good. With their mutual appreciation of the arts and their imaginative and creative natures they have many interests in common. They also both know how to enjoy themselves and like to live well. The Snake and Goat are often connoisseurs of good food and drink and they pass many a happy hour in each other's company. They understand each other well and can become firm friends.

The Snake and Goat also work well together and, if their work is of a creative nature, they may enjoy much success. In their work the Goat benefits from the Snake's wise counsel and quiet determination, while the Snake gains from the Goat's inventive and original mind. There is a good rapport between them, although they need to exercise care when dealing with finance. Both signs can be indulgent and, without a certain discipline, they may find their spending quickly depletes any profits they make.

In the parent–child relationship the Goat child responds well to his quiet and loving Snake parent and values the security, tranquility and comfort of a Snake home. There is a good bond between them. When the Goat is parent and the Snake the child, the Snake child delights in the kindly and affectionate ways of a Goat parent, although may sometimes feel unsettled by the capriciousness of his parent. However, the Snake child is a great source of pride to the Goat and they enjoy a good rapport.

In Love and Marriage

The Snake and Goat are often attracted to each other and in love and marriage they can find much happiness. Both signs have a quiet and easygoing disposition and feel comfortable in each other's company. Neither likes to live in a fraught or frenzied atmosphere and, as far as possible, they strive to maintain a happy equilibrium. They also share many interests, particularly of an artistic nature, and together they may enjoy music, literature, the theatre or some other aspect of the arts. They also have a fond appreciation of the finer things in life and aim to lead a comfortable, leisurely and even luxurious existence. The one problem that could beset them is that both can be indulgent and, despite the Snake's financial acumen, their money and savings may be quickly spent. In a match between the Snake and Goat there needs to be a tight control over the purse strings.

Although the Snake may at times despair over the Goat's

capricious nature, they do support and encourage each other in their various endeavours. The Goat draws strength from the Snake's quiet and determined manner, while the Snake appreciates the originality, imagination and artistic talents of the Goat. There is much love and accord between them and, with their fondness for the good things in life, their relationship is likely to be fulfilling and enjoyable. In love and marriage they are well suited.

SNAKE AND MONKEY

General Relations

On a social level the Snake and Monkey can get on reasonably well. Although they have different temperaments – the Snake being quiet and placid and the Monkey more lively and outgoing – there is considerable respect and liking between them. The Snake enjoys the Monkey's sparkling company and is enchanted by the Monkey's lively and resourceful nature, while the Monkey values the Snake's calm and thoughtful ways. Each has qualities that the other admires and they learn much from each other. Their interests may not always coincide, but they always have time for each other and can become good friends.

When the Snake and Monkey work together relations between them may prove difficult. The Snake is thoughtful, cautious and calculating, while the Monkey is geared up for action. The Monkey may view the Snake as a restraining influence, while the Snake considers the Monkey over-hasty and too impulsive. Both can be evasive and secretive and they are more likely to keep their ideas and plans to themselves rather than co-operate or work closely together.

In the parent–child relationship the Monkey child delights in the love and care that the Snake parent gives. The Snake parent does much to encourage the Monkey's keenness to learn and guide him in his many interests. The Monkey child is inquisitive and versatile and a Snake parent helps the Monkey child to make the most of his many abilities. There is a good rapport between them. When the Monkey is parent and the Snake the child, relations may not be so easy. The quiet and reserved Snake child may at times feel overwhelmed by the vitality of a Monkey parent. The Monkey parent really needs to understand the complex and often demanding ways of a Snake child. Once this has been achieved and they can accommodate each other's personalities, then the relationship between them may become close and loving.

In Love and Marriage

The Snake and Monkey are two of the most complex signs in the Chinese zodiac; the Snake because he keeps his thoughts and emotions so close to his chest, while the Monkey is an expert at concealing his feelings behind his genial and personable nature. It is perhaps because of their complexity that the Snake and Monkey intrigue each other and are drawn together. Once entwined, they rarely separate. In love and marriage the Snake and Monkey complement each other well and can form a loving and enduring relationship.

In a Snake–Monkey match each benefits from the qualities and skills of the other. The Snake delights in the Monkey's ebullient manner and marvels at the Monkey's resourcefulness. The Monkey inspires and motivates the Snake and helps make the Snake become more outwardly confident. The Snake is, however, more reflective and cautious than the Monkey and is a useful check on the Monkey's impulsive and sometimes reckless notions. The Monkey values the Snake's advice and opinions and they go through life helping, supporting and encouraging each other. Both are intelligent, gifted in many different areas and find each other stimulating company. Their social life also gives both much pleasure and between them they are likely to have many friends. Both also have a good sense of humour and there is likely to be much laughter and enjoyment in their relationship.

Generally, relations between the Snake and Monkey are good, but both partners also need to make adjustments in order for them to live in harmony. The Monkey needs to recognize that the Snake cannot be hassled or hurried against his will, so in this respect the Monkey needs to be more patient. Similarly the Snake, usually so possessive, needs to allow the Monkey a certain liberty and freedom to pursue his own interests. The Monkey, while remaining loyal, still cherishes his independence. If they can recognize these possible problem areas, the Snake and Monkey can form a happy and long-lasting relationship. Any children that they have help unite them further.

With care, and a certain adjustment on both sides, the Snake and Monkey make a good match. They complement each other well.

SNAKE AND ROOSTER

General Relations

These two signs admire each other emormously. They have a good rapport and understanding and general relations between them are good. Both have keen and penetrating minds and find that they are intellectually well matched. They enjoy each other's company and delight in the many lively conversations and discussions that they have. Socially the Snake and Rooster can become firm and loyal friends and both gain much from their friendship.

The Snake and Rooster can also form a successful working partnership, with each benefiting from the skills of the other. The Rooster is the more outgoing and pushy of the two and inspires and motivates the Snake as well as prodding the sometimes over-cautious Snake into action. However, the Rooster gains from the Snake's considerable business acumen and is reassured by the Snake's calm and determined nature. Both signs are ambitious and together can enjoy much success. Both may need to curb their sometimes indulgent natures, thought, and not dip into their profits too often.

In the parent–child relationship it does not matter which sign is parent and which child. In both combinations there is a strong bond between parent and child. They understand each other well and both Snake and Rooster children benefit from the attentiveness of their Snake or Rooster parent, as well as valuing the order and security found in a Snake or Rooster home. The child strives to live up to the parent's expectations and is a source of much pride.

In Love and Marriage

The Snake and Rooster are attracted to each other and are well suited. They complement each other well and in love and marriage both gain much from their relationship.

Unlike some signs, the Snake understands the Rooster well. Behind the Rooster's often blustering exterior there lurks a wonderfully rich and warm personality and it often takes a quiet and perceptive sign such as the Snake to appreciate the Rooster as he is rather than as he appears. The Snake loves and admires the Rooster and places much faith and trust in him. In addition to the splendid rapport that they have, the Snake delights in the efficiency of a Rooster partner. The Rooster is methodical, a super organizer, a great homemaker and is also extremely reliable. Furthermore, the Rooster is loyal and faithful, two qualities that are most important to the possessive Snake.

Just as the Snake values the many virtues of the Rooster, so too the Rooster appreciates the quiet, kind and attentive nature of the Snake. The Rooster delights in the Snake's keen intellect and conversational skills as well as his determined and ambitious nature. Both signs support and encourage the other and bring out the best in their partner. Admittedly each also has traits the other may dislike. The Snake may despair of the Rooster's fussiness and vanity, while the Rooster may be irritated by the Snake's sometimes evasive and secretive nature. But these are minor hurdles. These two signs mean much to each other and, with their smart and elegant appearance, they can make a striking and attractive couple. The Snake and Rooster are highly compatible and in love and marriage can find much happiness.

Snake and Dog

General Relations

The Snake and Dog both choose their friends with care and it is often some while before either is prepared to lower his reserve and let others into his confidence – and so it is when these two signs meet. Relations are initially cool as they test each other out. But in time the Snake and Dog can develop a good understanding and grow to trust and like each other. The Dog learns to appreciate the Snake's wise and reflective ways, while the Snake admires the Dog's integrity and magnanimous nature. In time they can become good and loyal friends.

When the Snake and Dog work together there may be loyalty between them, but not always complete accord. The Snake is ambitious and determined and likes to do things in his own way and own time. The Dog, however, needs to feel motivated and inspired before he can give of his best, and his anxious and sometimes pessimistic nature may unnerve the otherwise cool Snake. There may also be a difference in outlook. The Dog is not as materialistic as the Snake and may be reticent about some of the Snake's actions and motives. The Snake and Dog may like each other and hold each other in high regard, but in business this does not necessarily make them the most effective of teams.

In the parent–child relationship the conscientious Dog parent is constantly worrying about the quiet and introverted ways of a Snake child. But this worry is misplaced. The Snake child is content to live in the protective influence of a Dog household and values the love and affection that the Dog parent bestows on him. When the Snake is the parent and the Dog the child, the child again benefits from the love, security and calm atmosphere found in a Snake home. The Dog child is conscientious, affectionate and strives to please his parents – and usually succeeds! In both cases, parents of these signs have good reason to be proud of their children.

In Love and Marriage

These signs mean much to each other and in love and marriage can find contentment together. However, for this to be so, adjustments need to be made and both need to show a willingness to compromise in times of difficulty.

The Snake is more ambitious and materialistic than the Dog. He seeks a secure and comfortable way of life and can sometimes become preoccupied with the pursuit of wealth, success and material comforts. While the Dog, too, values security and stability, the Dog often disapproves of the Snake's materialistic and mercenary attitude. This difference may lead to misunderstanding and tension between them. Also, the Dog tends to be a worrier and can suffer from bouts of anxiety. While the Snake may sympathize, he may not fully understand the workings of the Dog's mind and may lose patience when the Dog is in one of his darker moods. Similarly, the Dog can be notoriously stubborn and this, too, causes annoyance to the more composed Snake.

Fortunately, both signs are usually able to recognize these problem areas and make every effort to adjust to each other. Also, both possess qualities that the other admires. The Snake, so possessive in his relationships, values the loyalty and dependability of a Dog partner, as well as appreciating the Dog's caring, attentive and discreet ways. Similarly, the Dog draws comfort from the Snake's calm, quiet and confident manner and admires his intelligence and wise counsel.

Provided the Snake and Dog can reconcile the differences that exist between them, then, in love and marriage, they can find happiness together. With care and understanding this can be a loving and reasonably good match.

SNAKE AND PIG

General Relations

The good-natured Pig gets on well with most signs, but the Snake may prove to be the exception. Snakes and Pigs do not relate well to each other and relations between them can be difficult. The problem lies in their different personalities. The Pig is honest and open towards others and he expects those he comes in contact with to be the same. However, the Snake can be reserved and secretive and the Pig may find it hard to penetrate through the Snake's evasive nature. The more the Pig may try to understand the Snake, the more evasive the Snake may become. The Pig does not understand the Snake's solitary nature and the Snake feels ill at ease with the Pig's open and easygoing manner. General relations between them are poor.

When the Snake and Pig work together relations between them may also prove tricky. Again the Pig is wary of the Snake's guarded manner and also finds the Snake a restraining and inhibiting influence. The Pig is far more action orientated than the Snake and the two generally set about their activities in different ways. The Snake is given to much planning and thought, while the Pig prefers to immerse himself straightaway in the action. There is a general lack of accord between them although, if they can overcome their differences, each may benefit from the other – the Pig from the Snake's planning and wise counsel and the Snake from the Pig's persistent and diligent manner. Their individual strengths could complement each other well, but first they need to build up their trust in each other.

In parent–child relationships between these signs, the Pig child values the quiet and secure atmosphere of a Snake home and endeavours to live up to the Snake parent's expectations. Both the Snake parent and Pig child have interests they can share and together can build up a good rapport. When the Pig is parent and the Snake the child, the Pig parent lavishes much care and attention on the Snake child, but is perplexed by the Snake child's sometimes aloof and distant manner. However, the Pig parent can take heart. Despite the Snake child's quiet and undemonstrative nature he loves his Pig parent dearly and appreciates the comfort and harmony of a Pig home.

In Love and Marriage

Snakes and Pigs have difficulty in relating to each other and in the early stages of any relationship there is some reserve and lack of accord. The Pig is puzzled by the Snake's reserved and guarded manner, while the Snake finds it hard to open up to the Pig's easygoing and good-humoured nature. The Pig is straightforward, the Snake complicated and it takes some time for each to come to terms with the other. A romance between these signs may go through some awkward and testing moments, but if they are prepared to persist, then it is just possible that they might begin to discover each other's more positive qualities.

In time the Pig learns to recognize the Snake's quiet and thoughtful nature and admires the Snake's wisdom and ambition. The Snake, in turn, values the integrity and trusting nature of the Pig. Also, the Snake benefits from the Pig's more outgoing and genial manner – all too often the Snake can withdraw into himself and be something of a loner, but, under the Pig's influence, the Snake may become more outwardly confident. Both have a fond appreciation of the good things in life and if finances permit – as they surely do, for both are skilled in financial matters – they can enjoy a comfortable and rather indulgent lifestyle.

The Pig may lack the refinement of the Snake and the Snake may not always be as forthcoming as the Pig would like, but if both partners are prepared to work hard at their relationship, then in love and marriage they could find a certain contentment. But it should be stressed that a Snake–Pig marriage may not be the easiest and it takes considerable effort and goodwill on both sides for the relationship to work. This is a challenging match and one which the Chinese generally advise against.

Horse and Horse

General Relations

The Horse enjoys company and he particularly enjoys the company of another Horse. They share many interests and have a similar outlook on life. Their love of conversation leads to some lively and spirited discussions and they spend many a happy hour in each other's company. There is a good rapport and understanding between them and two Horses can become close and loyal friends.

In his work the Horse is diligent, enterprising and industrious and by combining their strengths, two Horses can form a strong partnership. They have the drive and enthusiasm to do well. However, if they are to make the most of their strengths, they should agree on a clear division of responsibilities and remain committed to a specific goal. Without this discipline between them, two Horses may well end up jockeying for control and competing with each other rather than working together. For the short to medium term, a two-Horse team may enjoy much success, but in time their independent natures may get the better of them and they may prefer to go their separate ways.

In the parent–child relationship the Horse parent is well placed to understand the ways of the Horse child. The parent does much to support and encourage the child's wide-ranging interests and there is a close bond between them. However, the Horse parent would do well to instil a certain discipline in the Horse child and encourage the child to persist in his various activities rather than going from one activity to the other. If the Horse parent can do this, then his Horse child will have learnt a valuable lesson. However, despite the closeness between parent and child, the Horse child is still intent on leaving home early and gaining the independence he so dearly seeks.

In Love and Marriage

When the Horse falls in love, he falls truly and deeply in love. There are no half measures. His passion and devotion to the source of his affection is complete. When it is to another lively and spirited Horse, his love knows no bounds. Certainly this is so in the early stages of their relationship.

Horses are very much attracted to each other and with their wide-ranging interests they find they have much in common. Horses like talking, socializing, travelling – indeed, they will have a whole multitude of interests they can share and together they have much fun. However, while there is so much in favour of a relationship between two Horses, problems can and do emerge.

The Horse has a temper and, although often short lived, many a Horse has said things he has later regretted. When two Horses are together their combined tempers may lead to some heated exchanges. Also, Horses can be restless as well as having an independent streak in their natures and without care this, too, may put strains on their relationship. Fortunately, though, the Horse is well placed to understand another Horse and ideally in their relationship each allows the other time to pursue and follow his own individual interests.

With care and understanding the Horse couple can find much happiness. They may have their differences, but they mean much to each other and, with their romantic and passionate natures, their many mutual interests and often similar outlooks, their life together can be active, fun and fulfilling. In love and marriage this can be a good match.

Horse and Goat

General Relations

Although the Horse and Goat have very different personalities they understand each other well. There is an excellent rapport between them and with their lively and sociable natures they enjoy each other's company. They are likely to share many interests, including a love of the countryside, travel and socializing. They trust and respect each other and the Horse and Goat often become close and lasting friends.

The Horse and Goat also work well as colleagues and business partners. Indeed, their different skills and strengths prove complementary and both gain much from the partnership. The Goat, who at times can be indecisive, happily leaves much of the decision making and running of the business to the Horse. The Goat admires the enterprise and sense of purpose of the Horse and the Horse is content to take the lead. However, should difficulties emerge, the Goat is always at hand to lend support and encourage the Horse and, just as important, bolster the Horse's ego. The Horse motivates and inspires the Goat and this enables the Goat to give of his best. Also, the Horse benefits from the Goat's imagination and creativity and the Goat supplies a valuable input of new ideas and suggestions into their work. There is trust and rapport between them and, with the right luck, their work together may prove successful.

In the parent–child relationship there is a close affinity between the parents and children of these signs. They love each other dearly, but this may still not prevent the occasional rift from occurring. The lively and spirited Horse child can be demanding – sometimes too demanding – of an easygoing Goat parent and this may cause the Goat parent some anxiety. Similarly, the Goat child's carefree attitude may perturb the Horse parent and again there may be clashes when the parent feels the Goat child is not doing enough. However, despite this, the parents and children relate well to each other, have many interests they can share and there is much affection between them.

In Love and Marriage

With their lively and sociable natures, the Horse and Goat are often drawn together and in love and marriage are well suited. They make a devoted and loving couple and their relationship has every chance of lasting. Horses and Goats understand each other well and their individual strengths and talents are often complementary. Both gain much from their relationship.

The Horse and Goat have many interests in common and are likely to lead an active and enjoyable social life. Between them they have a large circle of friends, are keen partygoers and entertainers, and as a couple they make perfect hosts. The Horse very much values the unfailing and unquestioning support of the Goat and the Goat is an expert at defusing the Horse's temper and of boosting the Horse's ego as and when the situation dictates. Unlike other signs, the Goat understands the Horse's swings in moods well and is adept at coping with them. The Horse also appreciates the Goat's artistic and creative talents and particularly the Goat's skills as a homemaker.

Similarly, the Goat greatly admires the Horse's strength of character and industry. The Horse works hard, is conscientious and sets about his activities with enterprise and enthusiasm. The Horse is a source of inspiration for the Goat and, under the Horse's protective and helpful influence, the Goat's confidence and self-esteem rise considerably. The Horse can often bring out the best in the Goat.

The Horse and Goat respect each other's advice and views and value the support that the other gives. They have much fun in their relationship and their life together is full and varied. The Horse and Goat make a splendid couple and, with their passionate and romantic natures, are ideally suited. This is an excellent match.

Horse and Monkey

General Relations

The Horse and Monkey tend to be wary of each other and, while their relations may be reasonable, they are unlikely to become close or firm friends. The Horse is suspicious of the wily and crafty nature of the Monkey, while the Monkey has problems relating to the strong and independent-minded Horse. They may enjoy a lively conversation once in a while and, with their versatile natures, find they have things in common, but there is a lack of trust and accord between them. General relations between them are never strong.

When the Horse and Monkey are colleagues and business partners their combined talents may bring them success. The Horse is industrious and hard working, while the Monkey is enterprising and resourceful. Both are versatile and intelligent and if they are to work together their achievements may be considerable. However, success could be blighted by their mistrust of each other. The honest and straightforward Horse does not tolerate the cunning and sometimes devious ways of the Monkey, while the Monkey is suspicious of the Horse's proud and independent attitude. To attain success, each needs to adjust their ways and become more trusting of the other, and this is something neither finds easy to do.

In a parent–child relationship relations between these signs are generally good, although not always harmonious. The Monkey parent delights in the diligence of a Horse child, but at the same time finds it hard to deal with the Horse's somewhat independent and self-willed nature. When the Horse is parent and the Monkey the child, the Horse parent marvels at the resourcefulness and versatility of the Monkey child, but may not be so appreciative of the Monkey's rather mischievous nature. One saving grace is that both Horses and Monkeys have so many interests that the parents and children of these signs invariably have interests they can cultivate and share.

In Love and Marriage

The Horse and Monkey have many traits in common. They are both strong-minded and outgoing signs. They are versatile, have many interests and set about their activities with verve and enthusiasm. However, they do not relate well to each other and in love and marriage their relationship may not be easy.

Part of the problem is that both these signs are so strong willed. Neither is prepared to give ground to the other and there is a continual tussle for authority and the last word. Although both may like talking, they do not really communicate or understand each other.

The Monkey can be secretive and evasive and is a master at concealing his true feelings, and this is something that irritates the Horse. If the Horse can be so open in expressing his feelings, why cannot the Monkey? The Horse also dislikes the Monkey's sometimes devious and opportunistic ways and, for one so honourable, this is something that the Horse finds hard to accept.

The Monkey recognizes and appreciates the Horse's loyalty and lively and conscientious manner, but has great difficulty in accepting that the Horse needs a certain independence and freedom. Similarly, the Monkey finds the Horse's quick temper and impatient attitude difficult to bear.

It takes an exceptional Horse–Monkey couple to make their relationship work, but fortunately there are such couples. Each has to go some way towards adjusting to the other and each partner also needs to allow the other the opportunity to develop his own interests, hobbies and career rather than insist on complete togetherness. If they can achieve this, then in love and marriage the Horse and Monkey can remain together as two lively, spirited and strong-willed individuals. But if this understanding cannot be reached, then the prospects for a harmonious and lasting union remain bleak.

Horse and Rooster

General Relations

Lively, quick witted and sociable, the Horse and Rooster enjoy each other's company. Together they happily attend social functions, have spirited discussions and generally enjoy themselves. For a time they can become good friends, although the long-term prospects may not be so favourable. Both the Horse and Rooster can be notoriously candid in their views and their forthright natures can easily get the better of them. Both are strong willed and neither gives way to the other. When there are things to do and everything is fine, the Horse and Rooster are great chums, but when things start to go wrong, the squabbling starts. General relations in the short to medium term are good; beyond that, poor.

Both the Horse and Rooster are hard workers and, as colleagues and business partners, they can enjoy much success. The Horse benefits greatly from the Rooster's organizational skills, while the Rooster gains strength from the Horse's willpower and industry. They motivate and support each other and, if the Horse can look after the finances – the Rooster does tend to spend his money more freely than the Horse – their business could prove successful. The main problem is that both are egotistical and both will be keen to take the credit for their achievements.

In the parent–child relationship relations between these signs can prove difficult. Both Horse and Rooster children can be self-willed and stubborn and this almost certainly leads them into conflict with their strict Horse or Rooster parent. Also, Horse and Rooster children are more independent than some, preferring to do things their own way rather than continually relying upon parental support and guidance; this, too, could prevent there being a particularly close relationship with their parents.

In Love and Marriage

The Horse and Rooster are often attracted to each other and, with their fine and elegant looks, can make a striking couple. They are both outgoing signs and have many interests in common. Both enjoy outdoor activities and may be keen gardeners and travellers and have a fondness for the country-side. They also enjoy conversation, like socializing and keep themselves busy with a whole range of activities. For a time the Horse and Rooster can be blissfully happy, but if they are to maintain their affection, they need to show some willingness to adjust to each other.

Both signs can be frank and forthright in expressing their views and, while each appreciates a certain amount of straight talking, this may easily spill into criticism. Without tact and restraint by both, relations between them may quickly become strained. Also, both the Horse and Rooster can be vain and egotistical and each tries to dominate the relationship. In a Horse–Rooster household it is best if they have a clear division of responsibilities.

They also need to reconcile their different natures. The Horse is more adventurous than the Rooster and likes to do things on the spur of the moment, while the Rooster likes to plan and set about his activities in a more orderly manner. At times the

Rooster despairs of the Horse's restlessness, while the Horse sometimes finds the Rooster inflexible and rather set in his ways.

There are undoubtedly problems that the Horse and Rooster face in their relationship but, with their many joint interests and the strong physical attraction that they feel for each other, they can, with care, still enjoy a lively and fulfilling relationship. They may also benefit from each other's strengths – the Horse from the Rooster's methodical and disciplined manner and the Rooster from the Horse's practical and enterprising nature – but both need to work hard at their relationship and show a willingness to adapt to the other. If they can do this, then as a couple they can find much happiness. This can be a good, although sometimes challenging, match.

HORSE AND DOG

General Relations

The Horse and Dog understand each other well and can become close companions and lifelong friends. There is respect and trust between them and each does much to help and support the other. They often share similar interests and feel comfortable in each other's company. Their different temperaments are well suited and there is a good rapport between them. Generally, relations between the Horse and Dog are excellent.

These two signs also work well together and, as colleagues and business partners, they make a powerful combination. Both work hard and both attach much importance to openness and honesty in their business dealings. There is trust and respect between them and each remains mindful of the other's views and advice. Of the two, the Dog may be the more cautious but is a useful restraining influence on some of the Horse's more rash and impulsive notions. However, the enterprising Horse does much to inspire and enthuse the Dog and together, with their individual skills and strengths, they make a good and often successful team.

In the parent–child relationship, there is much love between these signs, but not always total accord. The dutiful Dog parent may worry over the Horse child's restless and independent-minded ways and, while the Horse child appreciates the love and guidance of the Dog parent, the child does so like to do things on his own – something a protective Dog parent may not always appreciate. When the Horse is parent and the Dog the child, the Dog child may not like the egotistical tendencies of his Horse parent, but will admire the Horse parent's integrity and vivacity. The Dog child strives to please the Horse parent and benefits from the Horse parent's wide interests and lively nature.

In Love and Marriage

The Horse and Dog are well suited and in love and marriage they can find much happiness. Not only is the physical attraction between them strong but they each have qualities that the other greatly admires. The Horse values the Dog's loving and affectionate ways and draws much strength from the Dog's unfailing support. In so many aspects of the Horse's life the Dog is caring, dependable and reliable – always there to advise, comfort and support.

The Dog, in turn, enjoys the Horse's liveliness, wit, intelligence and his outgoing and sociable nature. The Horse does much to lift the Dog's spirits and is also able to effectively dispel some of the anxieties and worries that so often beset the Dog. The Dog recognizes the Horse's need for a certain independence and allows the Horse time to pursue and cultivate his own interests. However, should the Horse ever wrong the Dog and take advantage of the Dog's trust, their otherwise close relationship could be damaged beyond repair. Horses, take note!

The Horse and Dog do, however, share many interests. They both like to keep themselves active and may have a particular fondness for outdoor activities such as gardening, travelling, and watching or taking part in sport.

As in so many things, the Horse and Dog go through life helping and supporting each other and theirs is a unique and special relationship. They understand each other superbly well and in love and marriage they make a splendid and devoted couple. They are highly compatible and make an excellent match.

HORSE AND PIG

General Relations

The Horse and Pig have a high regard for each other and general relations between them are usually good. Both have outgoing and sociable natures and they enjoy each other's company. As friends they lead an active social life and share many interests. Both can be witty and high spirited and theirs is an easygoing and fun relationship. Provided the more dominant Horse does not try to impose his will too strongly on the Pig – which the Pig will thoroughly resist – the Horse and Pig can become good and loyal companions.

The potential also exists for a good working relationship. The Pig is an astute businessperson and skilful at making money, while the Horse is diligent and hard working. If, as colleagues and business partners, they can pool their talents and work towards a common objective they can do well. The Horse benefits from the Pig's more persistent and patient manner, while the Pig values the Horse's enthusiasm and enterprise. Both are also honourable and open in their business dealings. Their talents and strengths can complement each other well, although each needs to remain mindful of the other and it is best if they have a clear division of responsibilities.

In the parent–child relationship there is generally good rapport and understanding between these two signs. When the Horse is parent and the Pig the child, the Horse parent delights in the Pig child's lively and genial disposition. Admittedly both have stubborn natures and this may lead to the occasional conflict, but generally there is much love and affection between them. When the Pig is parent and the Horse the child, the Pig parent does much to encourage the Horse child's many talents and allows the child some independence and the freedom to cultivate his own interests. The Horse child appreciates this and is warm and loving towards his Pig parent, but this still does not stop him from leaving home at an early age.

In Love and Marriage

The Horse and Pig are often attracted to each other and, in love and marriage, they can form a close, loving and rewarding relationship. Not only is the physical attraction strong – both the Horse and Pig are passionate and sensual signs – but they understand and relate well to each other.

Both the Horse and Pig have outgoing and lively natures. They like to live life to the full and invariably keep themselves busy with a multitude of interests and an active social life. Between them they have many friends. Both also know how to enjoy themselves – the Pig can be indulgent and the Horse can be a spendthrift – and, providing their money lasts, a fair proportion of their time is spent in the agreeable pursuit of pleasure. It is perhaps fortunate that both have considerable earning abilities and that the Pig is usually fortunate in his financial affairs.

These two signs also appreciate each other's talents. The Pig is a good homemaker and, while the Horse may not be as home orientated as some, the Horse nevertheless values the comfort and agreeable surroundings that the Pig unfailingly creates. The Horse values the Pig's sincerity, integrity and good-humoured nature. The Pig is both reliable and dependable and can be a useful check on the Horse's restless and impulsive nature. The Pig, in turn, admires the Horse's strength of character and his lifely and enterprising nature.

Generally this is a rewarding relationship. However, the Pig, who values companionship so much, must allow the Horse time for his own interests rather than insist on complete togetherness in everything they do. The Horse needs his liberty and freedom. Similarly, the Horse must not try to take advantage of the relaxed and easygoing ways of the Pig and regard it as a sign of weakness. If the Horse tries to dominate the relationship, the Pig will resist in no uncertain terms. Theirs is a relationship made up of equals and the Horse must never be allowed to forget this.

In love and marriage the Horse and Pig are well suited and can form a close and loving relationship. A good match.

Goat and Goat

General Relations

Bright, sociable and often carefree, the Goat enjoys the company of another Goat. Together they have much in common and both are likely to share artistic interests. They also have a fond appreciation for the good life and, providing finances permit, invariably enjoy a fine meal together or attending some lavish function. Goats know how to enjoy themselves and general relations between them are invariably good.

In a working situation two Goats can work well together. They trust and respect each other and, if their work is of a creative nature, their joint skills could bring them considerable success. Goats also possess highly original and creative minds and a Goat twosome may generate some brilliant and innovative ideas. Admittedly the Goat is not the most commercially minded of signs, but in a working situation Goats support and inspire each other and, with the right luck, they may do well. However, as both can be indulgent, they need to exercise some discipline when dealing with the financial aspects of any concern.

In the parent–child relationship, the Goat parent and Goat child can strike up a marvellous rapport and their love for each other is strong and enduring. The Goat child is truly content in the harmonious atmosphere of a Goat household, and who better to understand the Goat child's artistic and imaginative leanings than another Goat? Although the Goat parent may not be a strong disciplinarian, the genial Goat child causes few problems. As parent and child, their relationship is truly special and valued by both.

In Love and Marriage

The Goat is an amorous, passionate and sensual sign and the attraction between two Goats is strong. With their sociable and easygoing natures they get on well together and can form a loving and close relationship.

Goats also know how to enjoy themselves and have a good appreciation of the finer things in life. Good food, wine, parties, socializing – these are all things that a Goat couple very much enjoy. They also both strive for a comfortable and secure existence. The Goat is a superb homemaker and their home is a veritable lovenest – exquisitely and tastefully furnished and full of the latest in home comforts. Between them they pour much energy into creating and setting up their home and both regard it as their own private and secure sanctuary – a protection from the outside world.

Both are likely to have strong artistic leanings and have similar interests, including a possible love of music, literature and the performing arts. Where creativity is involved, each Goat does much to encourage the other and their combined talents often work well together.

However, while two Goats are well matched, problems can arise. The Goat tends to spend his money freely, and when two Goats are together there may be little control over the purse strings. The spending habits of two Goats can quickly deplete any savings they have. Also, when problems arise, the Goat can be a pessimist and when two Goats are downhearted they may have difficulty in lifting each other's spirits. In addition, Goats have capricious natures and this, together with moments of stubbornness, may cause tension between them. Fortunately, though, many Goat couples are quick to detect problem areas and as neither likes unpleasantness or scenes, most of the difficulties that do arise are quickly swept aside.

Providing the Goat couple exercise care with their finances, they can form a loving, secure aı d harmonious relationship. In love and marriage, a Goat couple are well matched.

Goat and Monkey

General Relations

The Goat and Monkey enjoy each other's company and relations between them can be good. Both are outgoing and sociable signs and find each other interesting and congenial company. They have a number of interests they can share and both are keen socializers. They respect and like each other and can become firm friends.

In a working situation the Goat and Monkey can get on well together. The Monkey appreciates the creative and inventive talents of the Goat, while the Goat recognizes the resourcefulness and enterprise of the Monkey. The Monkey does much to enthuse and motivate the Goat and, when they are united in pursuing a specific goal, their original and enterprising ways can lead them to success. There is a good level of respect and trust between them, although the more security-conscious Goat may not be so keen a risk taker as the Monkey.

In the parent–child relationship there is also an excellent rapport between these signs. The homeloving Goat child marvels at the versatility of his Monkey parent – whenever there are questions to be answered, problems to be solved or projects afoot, the Monkey is there to support, encourage and advise. The Goat child loves and trusts the Monkey parent – so much so that when the Goat decides to leave the delightful atmosphere of a

Monkey home it may prove a real wrench. Similarly, the resourceful and outgoing Monkey child thoroughly appreciates the love and care of a generally easygoing Goat parent. The Goat parent does much to encourage the Monkey's inquisitive, imaginative and versatile nature and together they share in much fun. To some, the parent–child relationships between these signs may seem unconventional, but there is a strong and enduring bond between them.

In Love and Marriage

Goats and Monkeys are often attracted to each other and their relationship is full of fun, variety and lots of love. Their witty, resourceful and inventive natures keep each other amused and there is much love and affection between them.

The Goat and Monkey also value each other's strengths. The Monkey appreciates the Goat's talents as a homemaker as well as the Goat's artistic and creative skills. The Monkey, who also possesses a creative mind, understands the Goat well and does much to help and encourage the Goat. Also, when the Goat is suffering from one of his more pessimistic moods, who better to raise the Goat's spirits than a lively and optimistic Monkey? The Monkey often brings out the best in the Goat.

Similarly, the Goat admires and is comforted by the resourcefulness and guile of the Monkey. Whenever there is a problem or a difficult decision to be made, the Monkey is there with a solution. The Monkey is marvellous company, is versatile, adaptable and, importantly for the Goat, a good provider. However, it is possible that the Goat may become increasingly dependent upon the Monkey and if this comes to be viewed by the Monkey as too much of a restraint the Monkey may become resentful and problems could emerge. Also, the Goat is much more of a romantic than the Monkey and the Goat's sensitive feelings could sometimes be hurt because the Monkey is not as open or as forthcoming in his declarations of love as the Goat may like.

Generally, however, the Goat and Monkey mean much to each other and they should be able to reconcile any difficulties that arise. By adapting to each other they may go through life enjoying themselves and having much fun. They never suffer from boredom or finding themselves with nothing to do. In love and marriage they can form a close and meaningful relationship.

GOAT AND ROOSTER

General Relations

The Goat and Rooster have very different personalities and viewpoints and relations between them can prove difficult. The Rooster is efficient, methodical and practical, while the Goat has a much more easygoing and carefree nature. The Rooster is disciplined and well organized; the Goat is not. The Rooster is also candid and forthright, while the Goat is wary of the some-times abrupt and matter-of-fact tones of the Rooster. The Goat and Rooster have little in common, do not fully understand each other and relations between them are often poor.

Their different outlooks also pose problems when these signs work together, either as colleagues or business partners. The Rooster is a hard and efficient worker, given to much planning and organization. The Goat, however, lacks the discipline of the Rooster and often needs motivation and encouragement before he is able to give of his best. The Rooster views the laid-back attitude of the Goat with disdain, while the Goat regards the Rooster's atti-tude as overbearing, pedantic and fussy. The only salvation is if their business is of a creative or artistic nature and the Rooster is able to manage the affairs of the Goat. With this one possible exception, there is little empathy between them and the Goat and Rooster find it hard to work satisfactorily with each other.

In the parent–child relationship again relations between the Goat and Rooster need careful handling. The Goat child needs much love, care and nurturing and may find the discipline and forthright nature of a Rooster parent hard to bear. When the Rooster is the child and the Goat the parent, the Rooster child may find the Goat's capricious and easygoing nature unappealing. The Rooster child appreciates order and routine, and this could well be lacking in a Goat household. Basically the general attitudes of the Goat and Rooster are very different and, regardless of the combination of parent and child, it takes much adjusting before they feel at ease with each other.

In Love and Marriage

The Goat and Rooster do not have much in common and have to make major adjustments if they are to enjoy a close and harmonious relationship. The difficulty lies in their very different attitudes. The Rooster is well organized, highly efficient and given to planning his activities with the utmost of care. The Goat, however, has a much more relaxed attitude to life and lacks the method and organization of the Rooster. In time the Rooster may find the Goat's attitude tiresome, while the Goat considers the Rooster too bound up in routine, pedantic and fussy.

The Goat is also more sensitive than the Rooster and all too often the Goat's feelings are upset by the Rooster's candid and forthright remarks. Similarly, the Rooster finds it hard to relate to the Goat's sometimes whimsical and fanciful nature and often despairs of the Goat's capriciousness. Some of the time these two signs could be operating on totally different wavelengths!

Another problem may arise over financial matters. Both signs can be free in their spending and, unless they are careful, the Goat and Rooster can quickly get through their savings and run into problems, putting yet another burden on their relationship.

It is, however, just possible that when the Goat and Rooster meet and fall in love they make every effort to adjust to each other.

This may not be easy, but it can be achieved – and, indeed, a relationship between the two may prove beneficial for both. The Rooster may become a more relaxed and diplomatic person under the Goat's guidance, while the Goat learns from the Rooster's more methodical and efficient ways. They may also further the joint interests that they have, notably a love of gardening, the countryside and socializing. But for the relationship to work, both partners need to show a willingness to adapt to the other. Also, the Goat tends to have a much more a norous nature than the Rooster and the Rooster needs to be more open in his affections to satisfy the Goat.

A lasting and harmonious relationship between these so very different signs can prove a challenge for both. But the challenge is there and if the Goat and Rooster's love for each other is strong enough then it is possible that they may make the adjustments needed to make their relationship work. Generally though, in love and marriage, this may prove a tricky match.

Goat and Dog

General Relations

There is little affinity between the Goat and Dog and general relations between these two signs are poor. They have few interests in common and their different personalities rarely gel. The capricious and whimsical Goat finds little favour with the more serious and dutiful Dog, while the Goat finds the Dog cynical, stubborn and idealistic. The Goat and Dog find it hard to build up a satisfactory rapport and both feel more at ease with some of the other signs in the Chinese zodiac.

This lack of accord is also apparent when the Goat and Dog are colleagues or business partners. To do well, both signs need encouragement and motivation, and this is something neither is able to provide the other. The Dog is distrustful of the Goat's capricious and somewhat laid-b. ck manner, while the Goat may find it hard to come to terms with the Dog's idealistic attitudes. Neither sign tends to be commercially minded and, as both can be worriers, should they encounter problems they are more likely to drown in a sea of anxiety and self-doubt than plan for survival. In business both need a more positive, assertive and optimistic partner and, in time, the Goat and Dog may well prefer to go their separate ways rather than struggle on together.

In the parent–child relationship a Goat child values the love and protection found in a Dog home, but the Goat child's whimsical and leisurely attitude may cause the dutiful Dog parent some concern. The Goat child often lacks the application and determination that the Dog parent feels he should have. When the Goat is parent and the Dog the child, the affectionate Dog child values the love and kindliness of a Goat parent, but could feel ill at ease with the capriciousness of his Goat parent. In both cases relations between the parent and child need to be handled with great care.

In Love and Marriage

Between them the Goat and Dog have many fine qualities. The Goat is kindly and good natured, while the Dog is loyal and attentive. But these signs also have weaknesses and when the Goat and Dog come together they seem to accentuate their negative traits. When the Goat and Dog fall in love they may find the road ahead pitted with difficulties.

The problem stems from their different personalities and outlooks. The Dog is far more serious than the more whimsical Goat. The Dog is an idealist and ever mindful of his duties and responsibilities. He can also be stubborn, obstinate and forthright and the Goat could have great difficulty in coming to terms with the character of the Dog. The Goat can be sensitive to the Dog's criticism and seeks a more active and lively existence than the Dog can provide. The Goat may appreciate the Dog's loyalty and affection, but does not always appreciate the Dog's viewpoints.

The Dog is, in turn, exasperated by the Goat's capricious and sometimes carefree manner. He has little appreciation of the Goat's imaginative and artistic nature and does not tolerate the Goat's whimsy. The Dog is direct, practical and matter of fact and the Goat is not. Their personalities are so different that agreement and understanding between then is at times difficult.

What traits they do share may only compound their difficulties. Both tend to be worriers and when problems occur they may both be beset with anxiety and together make a truly melancholy pair. Also, as both tend to spend freely, without care, they may face financial problems.

It takes a very special Goat–Dog couple to make their relationship work. Fortunately there are such couples and, providing each is prepared to go some way in adapting to the other, then they could develop a meaningful relationship. The Goat and Dog can learn much from each other and benefit from their different qualities – the Dog may become more relaxed in his attitude and the Goat become more objective. But generally, despite their many individual qualities, these two signs are not that compatible. A difficult match.

GOAT AND PIG

General Relations

The Goat and Pig are lively, sociable and good-natured signs and can get on well together. Not only do they enjoy an active social life, but their different personalities prove complementary. The Goat feels at ease and secure with the genial yet robust Pig, while the Pig enjoys the Goat's easygoing nature. They can strike up a good rapport and often become firm and trusted friends.

The Goat and Pig also work well together. Again their different personalities and skills complement each other and, as colleagues or business partners, they make a successful combination. The Goat benefits from the commercial acumen and money-making talents of the Pig, while the Pig values the Goat's imagination and creative skills. In such a partnership the Goat often provides the ideas, while the Pig has the drive and expertise to put the ideas into practice. They help, motivate and inspire each other and again there is good rapport and trust between them. This is a most effective partnership.

In the parent–child relationship there is always much love between these signs. The Goat parent enjoys the amiable and affectionate ways of a Pig child and as the Pig child is usually undemanding, gives the Goat parent few problems. Similarly, the Goat child enjoys a good rapport with the Pig parent and feels loved and secure in the harmonious atmosphere of a Pig household. In both cases the children of these signs flourish under the love and care of a Goat or Pig parent.

In Love and Marriage

The Goat and Pig are two signs that know how to enjoy themselves. Both like socializing, have genial and friendly natures and a fondness for the good life. In love and marriage they are ideally suited.

The Goat and Pig both have amorous and sensual natures and often fall for each other. There is a great physical attraction between them and their sex life is active and fulfilling. Their personalities are also highly compatible. Both have generally placid temperaments and aim for a harmonious and stress-free existence.

The Goat, who seeks a resourceful and loving mate, is certainly not disappointed by the Pig. The Goat feels secure and at ease with the Pig as well as appreciating the Pig's many talents. The Pig is a skilful businessperson and is usually fortunate in money matters and this is something that the Goat very much appreciates. The good-natured Pig does much to ease many of the Goat's worries as well as being reasonably tolerant of the Goat's capriciousness.

The Pig, in turn, not only values the support, love and affection of the Goat, but also the Goat's expert skills as a homemaker. The Pig encourages and understands the creative and artistic talents of the Goat as well as enjoying the Goat's sense of whimsy. Between them they put much effort into their home and help each other with their various activities. They have a large number of friends and as a couple make perfect hosts and entertainers. Both strive for a harmonious atmosphere in their home; neither likes arguments, unpleasantness or discord.

The Goat and Pig work very much as a team and often bring out the best in each other. There is a good rapport and understanding between them and in love and marriage they can find much happiness. They are well suited and make an excellent match.

Monkey and Monkey

General Relations

With such a friendly and personable nature, the Monkey makes friends with considerable ease and who better to win his admiration and friendship than another sociable Monkey? Monkeys get on famously well with each other and general relations between them are usually excellent. Together they become accomplices, spurring and encouraging each other on to better and greater things. They can become great friends and marvellous companions.

In business few doubt the Monkey's flair and ability. The Monkey is resourceful, versatile and adept at solving problems, and usually enjoys considerable success in business matters. However, when two Monkeys work together as colleagues or business partners, a certain discipline is needed to make the relationship work. For all his many talents, the Monkey has an extremely competitive streak and often strives to go one better than the rest – and this includes trying to outwit another Monkey! If both Monkeys can resist the temptation to get the better of their partner then their combined strengths may bring them much success. But if not, the rivalry between them may undermine their partnership.

In the parent–child relationship the Monkey parent and Monkey child have a marvellous rapport. The Monkey parent does much to encourage the child's enquiring mind and helps him with his many interests. For many Monkey parents, having a Monkey child is a good excuse to relive some of the wonder, fun and excitement of their own Monkey childhood. The Monkey parent and child understand each other well and there is a considerable empathy between them. There is much love and fun in their relationship.

In Love and Marriage

There is a strong attraction betw en two Monkeys and, in love and marriage, they enjoy a happy, harmonious and close relationship.

Monkeys understand each other well and can build up a good rapport. They have many interests, some of which they share, but some that they happily continue on their own. Monkeys also recognize a need for a certain independence and freedom in their relationship and this they allow each other. Neither insists on complete togetherness in everything they do and there is much trust in their relationship.

They also do much to encourage and support each other. Monkeys make shrewd and wily advisers and, with the support of another Monkey behind them, both may go far. They are also skilful at making money and a Monkey couple should be materially well off – even though both can be indulgent.

Monkeys also like to keep themselves active and their life together is full of variety, new challenges and lots of fun. They like socializing, enjoy travelling and have a thirst for adventure and there is always something going on – life is never dull in a Monkey household!

The Monkey couple also take great pride in any children they have and make loving and caring parents. Monkeys enjoy parenthood and between them devote much time and energy to their children.

Monkeys have a knack in bringing out the best in each other and together they make an ideal couple. In love and marriage Monkeys are well suited and make a splendid match.

Monkey and Rooster

General Relations

The Monkey and Rooster are two forceful and outgoing signs and generally do not get on well together. The Monkey is a lively and high-spirited individual who likes to retain a certain amount of freedom in his actions, while the Rooster is more disciplined and much more conservative in outlook. The Rooster views the Monkey as an impetuous and undisciplined character, while the Monkey has little time for the Rooster's pedantic ways or forthright nature. They share few interests and have little understanding of each other. General relations between these two signs are usually poor.

This lack of rapport is also evident when the Monkey and Rooster are colleagues or business partners. Their approach to their work is often very different. The methodical and efficient Rooster likes to plan and organize his activities, while the Monkey is more of an opportunist and relies a lot on his charm and wits. The Rooster is distrustful of the Monkey's wily and sometimes crafty nature. There is little trust between them and unless they can unite in a common purpose, they quickly go their separate ways.

Relations are, however, much better in the parent–child relationship and both the Monkey and Rooster child will gain much from his parent. The firm but kindly Rooster parent is good discipline for the lively Monkey child but at the same time is keen to encourage the Monkey child's versatility and thirst for knowledge. There is a good bond between them, although the Rooster must never *ever* try to extinguish the Monkey child's sense of fun. When the Monkey is parent and the Rooster the child, the Rooster child relates well to the Monkey parent. The Rooster child appreciates the versatility, intellect and resourcefulness of the Monkey parent and strives to live up to his parent's expectations. The gifted Rooster child rarely disappoints and there is much respect and affection between them.

In Love and Marriage

With their outgoing and sociable natures, the Monkey and Rooster may be drawn together. The Rooster finds the Monkey lively and fascinating company, while the Monkey appreciates the style and self-assuredness of the Rooster. For a time they may get on well, particularly as both like partying and socializing. But their love and admiration for each other may be hard to maintain and in love and marriage the outlook may be bleak.

The problem lies in their very different natures. The Monkey is quick witted and resourceful and likes to retain a certain independence in his actions. The Rooster, however, is a great planner and organizer – not only of his own activities but of those around him – and this is something that the Monkey may find hard to accept. The Monkey is more action oriented and more spontaneous than the Rooster and he may find the Rooster a restraining influence. Nor does he care for the Rooster's forthright and candid manner. The Rooster, in turn, will be irritated by the Monkey's sometimes evasive and crafty nature and also consider him too materialistic in outlook.

As both are so strong minded and set in their ways, they may find compromise difficult and neither may be prepared to make the adjustment needed to suit the other. Generally, despite their many fine individual qualities, these two signs do not get and it takes an exceptional couple to make this relationship work. In love and marriage this is a difficult match.

Monkey and Dog

General Relations

There are many differences in outlook between the Monkey and Dog and, on a casual basis, relations between them may prove difficult. The altruistic Dog does not care for the self-seeking and opportunistic ways of the Monkey, while the Monkey finds the Dog a little too idealistic and unyielding for his liking. Both view the other with misgivings and general relations between them may be poor. However, if each is prepared to get to know the other better, then they begin to appreciate each other's finer qualities and relations between them improve. With goodwill and understanding on both sides, both could gain much from any friendship that develops.

When the Monkey and Dog work together, either as colleagues or business partners, they gain from each other's strengths. The Monkey is more enterprising and commercially minded than the Dog, while the Dog tends to be more disciplined and persistent than the Monkey. If they can unite in pursuing a specific goal, then the Monkey and Dog can enjoy much success, although the more honourable Dog may not be too keen on some of the Monkey's more crafty ploys.

In the parent–child relationship, there is much love and affection between the Monkey and Dog, although there may not always be complete understanding. The dutiful Dog parent is proud of the Monkey child's keenness and ability to learn, but may not be so appreciative of the Monkey's mischievous and lively ways. When the Monkey is the parent and the Dog the child, the Monkey parent does much to dispel some of the anxieties that so often concern the Dog child, but must not forget that the Dog child needs much in the way of protection and support and cannot always be left to his own devices, as the Monkey parent may sometimes think.

In Love and Marriage

While initial relations between the Monkey and Dog may be reserved and cool, the closer they draw together the better they appreciate each other's strengths and qualities. In time, and with some adjustments, the Monkey and Dog can form a satisfactory and loving relationship.

Each benefits from the qualities found in the other and in many respects their different strengths compensate for the weaknesses in the other. The more lively and spirited Monkey does much to alleviate some of the worries that beset the anxious and sometimes pessimistic Dog. The Dog also benefits from the Monkey's lively and sociable nature. Under the Monkey's influence the Dog becomes more relaxed, outgoing and flexible in outlook – all of which is to the Dog's advantage.

The Monkey also gains from the Dog. Not only does the Monkey value the loyalty and affection of a Dog partner, but comes to view the Dog as a trusted ally. The Dog is sincere, well meaning and thoughtful and the Monkey values the Dog's judgement. The Dog may also make the Monkey less materialistic in outlook and less self-centred. The Dog's strong ethical standing rubs off on the Monkey and the Monkey becomes more open and honourable in his dealings rather than so reliant on his wits. The Dog provides support, encouragement and love for the Monkey – all things that the Monkey values.

In love and marriage the Monkey and Dog need to allow time to adjust to each other and to modify their ways. Admittedly there may still be problems – both are cynical and there are times when the Dog becomes exasperated by the Monkey's restlessness or the Monkey despairs of the Dog's stubbornness – but these problems can be surmounted. If the Monkey and Dog have a family, this unites them further and both make proud and attentive parents.

As a couple they do much to help each other. Both are supportive and encouraging and, providing they can adjust to their different natures, the Monkey and Dog can find happiness together. In love and marriage they complement each other well.

Monkey and Pig

General Relations

The Monkey and Pig are both lively, outgoing and sociable signs and can get on extremely well together. There is a good understanding and rapport between them and they can become firm friends. They learn much from each other and both the Monkey and the Pig also tend to bring out the better qualities in the other. The Pig admires the confident and resourceful nature of the Monkey, while the Monkey values the sincerity and trust of the Pig. There is a genuine liking between them and general relations are good.

The Monkey and Pig also work well together, both as colleagues and business partners. Both recognize and value each other's strengths and there is co-operation and trust between them. The Monkey values the Pig's ability to work hard and his money-making talents, while the Pig draws strength and inspiration from the zest and enterprise of the Monkey. Also, under the Pig's watchful eye, the Monkey is prevented from carrying out some of his more crafty notions and this may well prove to be in the Monkey's interests. While the Monkey is not above duping others, the Monkey holds the Pig in too high a regard to trick his porcine partner. This can be a successful and profitable partnership for both.

In the parent–child relationship, relations between these two signs is again good. The Monkey child feels secure in the amiable and harmonious atmosphere of a Pig home, while the Pig child delights in the versatility and enthusiasm of the

Monkey parent. In both cases the child learns much from his Monkey or Pig parent and the parents have good reason to be proud of their Monkey or Pig child. There is a close bond between parent and child and there is much love and a good element of fun to the relationship.

In Love and Marriage

With their warm, friendly and sociable natures, the Monkey and Pig are often attracted to each other and can form a loving and harmonious relationship.

Although their outlooks may at first be different, both Monkey and Pig are adaptable and their love and high regard for each other enables them to make the adjustments necessary to live in harmony.

Together they cultivate and further their joint interests and, with their multitude of friends, enjoy an active social life. The Monkey readily appreciates the Pig's skills as a homemaker as well as delighting in the Pig's genial disposition. There is much good-humoured fun between them and great understanding. The Pig feels inspired by the enthusiasm of the Monkey, while the Monkey is reassured by the love and loyalty of the Pig. Each does much to support and encourage the other.

The more honourable Pig may, however, disapprove of the Monkey's more scheming and opportunistic ways, but under the Pig's influence the Monkey may well change for the better and become more open in his dealings and outlook. The Monkey may also become less self-centred. Similarly, the Monkey is a good adviser for the sometimes naïve and gullible Pig. Some Pigs also lack a competitive spirit or have insufficient drive to make the most of their many talents and the Monkey helps the Pig overcome this.

Both learn and gain from the other and in love and marriage they can develop a close and lasting relationship. This can be a beneficial match for both signs.

ROOSTER AND ROOSTER

General Relations

The Rooster is a lively and proud individual who picks his friends with care. While he may recognize many of his own qualities in another Rooster, his forceful and domineering nature gets the better of him and prevents two Roosters from ever becoming close or lasting friends. The Rooster likes to be in charge and have his own way and such an attitude leads to conflicts with another equally strong-minded and opinionated Rooster. They are both forthright and candid in expressing their views and again the result is much bickering and arguing. Generally when the Rooster meets another Rooster their strong and abrasive personalities clash and general relations between them are poor.

When two Roosters are colleagues or business partners again difficulties arise. Each wants to organize and command the other and each wants their own way. Neither gives way easily and rather than working together they are more likely to end up competing against each other. Between them they could set themselves unrealistic targets or get embroiled in so much detail that they do not make the most of their abilities. On his own, or with a more compatible partner, the Rooster can be particularly successful in business, but two Roosters together just clash and squabble – not a happy or successful combination.

There is trouble, too, when both the parent and child are Roosters. The Rooster parent tends to be strict and firm and likes to keep the house neat, orderly and running efficiently. Should a strong-minded Rooster child step out of line or speak out of turn, clashes ensue. The Rooster parent loves the Rooster child dearly and guides him well in his various activities, but the love that exists between them does not always come through. This is a difficult relationship.

In Love and Marriage

Roosters have many admirable qualities but when two Roosters get together their personalities clash and, rather than bringing out the positive qualities in each other, they invariably end up squabbling and competing with each other. Neither finds compromise easy and each tries to get the upper hand. The Rooster has an extremely competitive streak and feels that only one can rule the roost.

Another complication is that the Rooster is born under the sign of candour and when two Roosters are together both speak their minds openly and forcefully, and arguments will be a regular occurrence. Both also tend to be spendthrift and a Rooster couple may, if they are not careful, find themselves in financial difficulties.

There are, of course, exceptions to the norm and it is just possible that two Roosters may make a success of their relationship. Ideally they should agree on a specific division of responsibilities – rather than interfere too much with each other's activities – but at the same time cultivate their joint interests. Roosters are often diligent homemakers and keen gardeners and their home and garden may provide a good focus for their attention. Roosters also enjoy socializing, partying and travel. Providing they maintain some joint interests and resist the temptation of being too critical of each other, then it is just possible their relationship may work. If it does, and with their good looks and proud, dignified appearance they make a striking couple.

Sadly, however, more times than not, when two Roosters are

together their forthright and abrasive natures come to the fore and mar their relationship. Two Roosters have difficulty in living under the same roof and in love and marriage a Rooster couple may find themselves continually battling for dominance and subjecting each other to their candid views. With the rare exception, this is a difficult match.

ROOSTER AND DOG

General Relations

These two signs are both strong willed and strong minded and generally do not get on well together. Both have traits that irritate the other and as both can be forthright in expressing their views, tempers readily fly. The Rooster dislikes the Dog's stubbornness and cynical nature, while the Dog finds the Rooster vain and egotistical. They have few interests in common and find it hard to establish a satisfactory rapport. General relations between them are poor.

In business their different outlooks again pose problems. For the Dog to realize his true potential he needs to feel inspired and motivated – and the Rooster is more likely to alienate him than win his trust. The Dog feels ill at ease with the Rooster's forceful manner and the precision-like way in which he plans his activities, while the Rooster may feel unnerved by the worrying and anxious nature of the Dog. When problems emerge, as they surely will, their forthright natures get the better of them and their partnership degenerates into arguments and bitter recrimination. As colleagues or business partners the Rooster and Dog rarely work well together.

There are also problems in the parent–child relationship. The Dog parent worries over the independent and self-willed nature of a Rooster child and while he is keen to encourage the child with his hobbies and interests, they may find it difficult to strike up a meaningful rapport. When the Rooster is parent and the Dog the child, the Dog child's sensitive nature may often be upset by a firm and forthright Rooster parent. The Dog, in his formative years, needs much love, understanding and gentle encouragement and may not feel totally at ease with his candid parent. In both cases much care is needed if the parents and children of these signs are to develop a satisfactory relationship.

In Love and Marriage

The Rooster and Dog have very different personalities; while, for some, personality differences can prove complementary and make up for weaknesses in the other, this is not always the case with these two signs. Their differences lead to conflict and should the Rooster and Dog fall in love and decide to marry, their relationship may be fraught with difficulties. In love and marriage this is a very challenging match.

Part of the problem lies in their opposing outlooks. The Rooster can be vain, opinionated and self-centred, while the Dog is more altruistic and disapproves of the egocentricity of the Rooster. Also the Rooster has a tendency to dominate and to impose his sense of order and routine upon others and the strong-minded Dog resents this. While the Dog, too, likes an orderly existence, he does not like being bossed around and he may feel that the Rooster, with his flamboyant and exuberant style, goes over the top, is over-fussy and too interfering. What is worse, the Dog tells the Rooster so! Both can be frank and forthright in expressing their views and, in such a match, bickering and arguments may be a frequent occurrence.

Similarly, the Rooster is not as tolerant or as sympathetic as some to the Dog's anxious and worrying nature. The Rooster is also frustrated by the Dog's stubbornness. Basically there are just too many conflicts between them to make for harmonious living.

Both the Rooster and the Dog have many admirable qualities, but often their assertive and forthright natures get in the way and they fail to appreciate each other's finer qualities. In love and marriage this is often a difficult and challenging match.

ROOSTER AND PIG

General Relations

The amiable and affable Pig gets on well with most and, while the Pig may dislike the egocentricity of the Rooster, he nevertheless has a sneaking admiration for the resolute and candid bird. Similarly, the Rooster warms to the genial and trusting disposition of the Pig and general relations between them are good although not necessarily close. However, the longer they know each other, the better they are able to appreciate each other's more positive qualities.

In business both the Rooster and Pig are hard working and if they are united in pursuing a specific goal they can make an effective combination. However, the more cautious Rooster may not feel totally at ease with some of the risks that the Pig takes, while the Pig may at times find the Rooster's attitude inflexible and restrictive. Both are honourable in their business dealings and, even though they may not always be in full agreement with each other, there is a good level of respect between them.

In the parent–child relationship the children of these two signs relate well to their Rooster or Pig parent and there is much love and affection between them. The Pig child benefits from the order and discipline of the Rooster parent and responds well to the parent's attentiveness and care. The Pig child is generally well behaved and is a source of much pride to the Rooster. When the Pig is parent and the Rooster the child, the Rooster child also benefits from a good-natured Pig parent. The Pig parent does much to encourage the inquisitiveness and curiosity of a Rooster child and guides him wisely.

In Love and Marriage

There is much attraction between the Rooster and Pig and, while the early days of their romance may not be smooth – both signs need time to adjust to each other – the longer their relationship continues, the better it becomes. In love and marriage these two signs make a fine couple and, while there are problems they need to address, both can gain much from their relationship.

The Pig is much more easygoing and tolerant than the Rooster and falls in with many of the plans and routines that the Rooster imposes upon his household. The Rooster is a greater organizer and having such an efficient and orderly partner may be of assistance to the Pig. Similarly, under the Pig's good-natured influence, the Rooster may lose some of the more reserved and inhibited sides of his nature and become more relaxed and open.

The Rooster also values the Pig's integrity and judgement. Both are hard workers and while they can do well in their separate careers (and it is best if they did remain separate) the Rooster readily appreciates the Pig's money-making talents.

As a couple these two signs are likely to have several interests that they can share. Both pour much time and energy into their home and may also share an interest in gardening as well as being keen socializers. Between them they have many friends.

There are, however, problems which arise from some of the more awkward aspects of their personality. The Rooster despairs of the Pig's stubbornness and sometimes earthy nature, while the Pig wishes that the Rooster were more diplomatic and tactful rather than being so candid and confrontational. However, both the Rooster and Pig mean much to each other and, in time, learn to adjust and adapt to each other. In love and marriage this can be a positive and beneficial match.

DOG AND DOG

General Relations

There is much camaraderie between two Dogs and general relations between them are good. Dogs trust and understand each other and have similar outlooks and views. There is also considerable co-operation between them and they do much to help and support each other. Two Dogs can become loyal and trusting friends, although given their sometimes pensive and anxious natures, their relationship could be a touch on the serious side.

When Dogs work together as colleagues or business partners, there is trust and respect between them but this does not necessarily lead to success. The Dog tends to be a worrier and when difficult decisions need to be taken, the Dog twosome may be fraught with anxiety and tension. To do well the Dog needs a resolute figure alongside him who can provide inspiration and motivation, and it is questionable whether a Dog partner can give this. If they are lucky, a Dog team could just possibly make it – especially if their work is of a humanitarian nature and material goals are not so important – but, generally, a working relationship between two Dogs may not be the best.

The parent–child relationship is, however, marvellous. Who better to understand a Dog child than a Dog parent? The parent loves the Dog child dearly and does much to encourage and support him and the dutiful Dog child strives to live up to the Dog parent's expectations. Theirs is a special, close and enduring relationship.

In Love and Marriage

Dogs are romantics and when two Dogs fall in love there is a great meeting of minds and hearts. A Dog devotes himself completely to his partner and 'n a relationship between two Dogs there is much love, trust and understanding.

As a couple they do much to help and encourage each other. They work as a team and their loyalty and devotion to each other is unquestioned. Together they cultivate joint interests and, with their practical natures, often content themselves in carrying out projects around their home and garden. They make caring and attentive parents and both may also have an interest in humanitarian matters. A Dog couple can find much happiness together, but there are still problems they need to address.

The Dog can at times be outspoken and forthright and there is a frequent airing of views in a Dog household. Also, the Dog can be cynical, stubborn and a worrier and if a Dog couple fall on bad times or face difficulties they could both become ridden with anxiety and pessimism.

Fortunately, though, Dogs are resilient and survivors and together a Dog couple can ride out any storms that confront them and learn from their experiences.

With their dutiful and serious natures there may not be an abundance of mirth in a Dog household, but there is much love and affection. Dogs are ideally suited to each other and in love and marriage they make a devoted and attractive couple.

DOG AND PIG

General Relations

The Dog and Pig admire and respect each other and can become good and lasting friends. The Pig is attracted by the Dog's loyal and unselfish nature, while the Dog likes the Pig's genial, kindly and sincere manner. There is considerable rapport and understanding between them and general relations between these two signs are invariably good.

These two signs also work well together, either as colleagues or business partners. Both are open and honourable in their business dealings and the Dog draws inspiration from the hardworking Pig. The Pig is the more enterprising of the two, but can also be gullible and the Dog does much to protect and support his partner and friend. The Dog may not be as materialistic or so profit driven as the Pig but there is still much respect and trust between them. Both benefit from the skills of the other and together can form a useful working relationship.

In the parent–child relationship relations between these two signs are again strong. The sometimes anxious Dog child gains much from having an easygoing and affectionate Pig parent and the Pig parent does much to defuse the Dog child's worrying nature and help the child to become more confident and self-assured. When the Dog is parent and the Pig the child, the child responds well to his affectionate and dutiful Dog parent and strives to please. There is a close bond between them and in both cases parent–child relations between these two signs will be good.

In Love and Marriage

There is much respect and understanding between the Dog and Pig and in love and marriage they are well suited. Each gains from the other and together can make a close, happy and lasting match.

The Dog and Pig have many interests in common and this may include a love of the countryside and gardening. Both also have strong humanitarian leanings and do much to support worthy and charitable causes. They also take pleasure in creating and maintaining their home and, while the Dog may not be so indulgent as the Pig, they ensure it is comfortably furnished and has a secure and homely atmosphere. If they have children, both make caring and loving parents and ensure that their children have a good upbringing.

There is a good rapport and understanding between them and each is very much devoted to the other. The warm-hearted Pig values the loyalty and sincerity of the Dog, while the Dog enjoys the easygoing company of the Pig. The Pig's genial temperament is a good antidote for son e of the worries and anxieties that beset the Dog and the Dog benefits from the Pig's kindly and good-natured ways. Similarly, the Pig values the dependability of the Dog and pays heed to the Dog's wise counsel, views and opinions. Sometimes the trusting Pig can be too trusting and the Dog makes a worthy protector.

As in most relationships there are problems they need to address. Both can be stubborn and obstinate. The Dog may find the Pig over-indulgent and sometimes lacking in refinement, while the Pig may find the Dog too carefree in his spending and also not care for the Dog's outspoken and sometimes cynical views.

Fortunately, though, none of these problems are insurmountable and both value their relationship so much that they make every effort to adjust to the other. Their love, loyalty and devotion is strong and together they can find much happiness and bring out the best in each other. In love and marriage they make a splendid match.

PIG AND PIG

General Relations

The warm, friendly and sociable Pig is one sign who knows how to enjoy himself and when two Pigs get together they can be assured of having a great time. Two Pigs together make good friends and fine companions and general relations between them are excellent. They also do much to help and support each other and invariably share the same views and outlooks. Their friendship is close, enduring and consists of much good fun and humour.

Two Pigs also work well together. The Pig is usually lucky in business and an astute money-maker and, when two Pigs combine their talents, either as colleagues or business partners, success is also certainly assured. Pigs are hard and honest workers and through sheer determination and willpower (particularly if either have suffered a setback) they are determined to secure their objectives and make the most of their talents. There is trust and understanding between them and in business they make an excellent combination.

There is also a close bond between the Pig parent and Pig child. The Pig child thrives in the loving and harmonious atmosphere of a Pig home. However, the Pig parent would do well to keep a watchful eye over the Pig child and make sure that he uses his talents purposefully rather than flitting from one activity to another. A little discipline may not come amiss but, given the great love and affection that exists between them, the

Pig child invariably strives to please his Pig parent. Theirs is a close relationship, which both very much value.

In Love and Marriage

Kindly, sociable and reliable, the Pig makes an ideal partner and two Pigs together can find much happiness and contentment. In love and marriage they are well suited and each is devoted to the other.

Pigs understand each other well and there is considerable empathy between them. They support and encourage each other and bring out the positive qualities in the other. The Pig often needs an understanding and encouraging partner to help him realize his potential and who better to appreciate this than another Pig?

Both are hard working and together devote much time and energy to setting up and maintaining their home. Pigs are very much home-loving creatures and invariably fit it with all the latest in comforts as well as giving their home a calm, stable and harmonious atmosphere. With their financial skills, a Pig couple should enjoy much financial security.

Pigs also know how to enjoy themselves and a Pig couple leads an active social life, have many friends and a wide range of interests. They can be indulgent and have a good appreciation of the finer things in life. They enjoy dining, partying and, with their passionate and sensual natures, enjoy an active sex life. A Pig couple live and enjoy life to the full!

The Pig can, however, have a stubborn streak in him and occasionally this can lead to problems between them. But, generally, Pigs strive for a harmonious and pleasurable existence and this is what most Pig couples secure. In love and marriage they are well suited and make an excellent match.

Summary of Relationships

Rat and Rat: Sociable, charming and loving – a happy and close relationship.

Rat and Ox: These two trust and understand each other well – a meaningful relationship.

Rat and Tiger: Active, enterprising and immensely resourceful, these two can, with care, get on well.

Rat and Rabbit: These two may feel ill at ease with each other. Tricky.

Rat and Dragon: Love, respect, trust, rapport – they have it all. An excellent relationship.

Rat and Snake: With similar views and outlooks they complement each other well – a good relationship.

Rat and Horse: Their strong wills and determined natures just clash. A distinct lack of accord.

Rat and Goat: They may be great socializers, but their personalities often clash. Difficult.

Rat and Monkey: Lively, resourceful and enterprising – they are almost made for each other. A great relationship.

Rat and Rooster: Strong minded and forthright, these two are continually on their guard – a challenging relationship.

Rat and Dog: These two like, trust and respect each other – a sound and often solid relationship.

Rat and Pig: With their sociable natures and many similar interests, these two get on well together.

Ox and Ox: Practical, strong willed and direct, these two understand and respect each other.

Ox and Tiger: Their different attitudes, outlooks and personalities invariably lead to disagreements and difficult relations.

Ox and Rabbit: Quiet, reserved and refined, these two are in tune with each other. They are well suited.

Ox and Dragon: Despite some admiration of each other's talents, their personalities and interests are so very different. Relations will be tricky.

Ox and Snake: Calm, reflective and cautious, these two understand each other well. Relations will be good.

Ox and Horse: Their strong wills, different interests and forthright natures may cause many problems between them.

Ox and Goat: Their different attitudes, outlooks and personalities may lead to many disagreements. There is little understanding between these two.

Ox and Monkey: Their different personalities and individual strengths are often complementary. There is good respect between them.

Ox and Rooster: Careful, orderly, meticulous and direct – these two are made for each other.

Ox and Dog: They may be loyal to each other, but understanding may not always be so easy.

Ox and Pig: With similar views and values these two relate well to each other.

Tiger and Tiger: Restless, volatile and individualistic – there are many hurdles for them to overcome.

Tiger and Rabbit: These two can learn much from each other. Their different strengths and qualities are often complementary.

Tiger and Dragon: Dynamic and enterprising, these two live life to the full – but not always harmoniously.

Tiger and Snake: These two live life at different speeds and in different ways. They have little in common.

Tiger and Horse: Active, adventurous and enterprising, these two get on well.

Tiger and Goat: They may sometimes have to tread carefully, but these two like and respect each other.

Tiger and Monkey:	They have interests they can share, but relations could still be tricky.
Tiger and Rooster:	Their strong wills and forthright natures may lead to problems.
Tiger and Dog:	These two learn and gain from each other. There is much respect between them.
Tiger and Pig:	With many joint interests and a high regard for each other, these two get on well.
Rabbit and Rabbit:	Sociable, well mannered and peaceable, the Rabbit feels at ease with another Rabbit. They can become good friends.
Rabbit and Dragon:	Thesee two recognize each other's qualities and can learn much from each other. With care and consideration, these two can get on well.
Rabbit and Snake:	Thoughtful, reflective and refined, these two understand each other well.
Rabbit and Horse:	Their different personalities, interests and views may lead to many problems. Relations will not be easy.
Rabbit and Goat:	Respect, trust and understanding – the Rabbit and Goat have it all. They get on marvellously well.
Rabbit and Monkey:	These two generally enjoy each other's company although in business, relations may be more tricky.
Rabbit and Rooster:	There are many differences these two need to overcome. Relations will be far from easy.
Rabbit and Dog:	There is much trust and respect between these two and they get on well.
Rabbit and Pig:	These two are in tune with each other. They are well suited.
Dragon and Dragon:	Lively, outgoing and enterprising, two Dragons can, with care, get on well.
Dragon and Snake:	They understand each other perfectly – a great combination.
Dragon and Horse:	There is much admiration between these two and, with care, they can get on well together.

Dragon and Goat: They may have some fun together and for a time get on well, but their friendship may be difficult to maintain.

Dragon and Monkey: Sociable, lively and enterprising, these two understand each other well and relations between them are often excellent.

Dragon and Rooster: These two complement each other admirably. They get on well.

Dragon and Dog: With different interests and outlooks, relations will prove difficult.

Dragon and Pig: Good understanding and respect. These two can get on well.

Snake and Snake: They may admire each other, but Snakes are so possessive hat problems could easily emerge.

Snake and Horse: These two can form a reasonably good understanding although their different outlooks could lead to problems.

Snake and Goat: Quiet, creative and peaceloving, the Snake and Goat enjoy each other's company. Relations will be good.

Snake and Monkey: Their different personalities can prove complementary and they learn much from each other.

Snake and Rooster: These two have a high regard for each other and relations between them are often excellent.

Snake and Dog: They may not always understand each other but they do recognize each other's finer qualities.

Snake and Pig: Their different outlooks and attitudes lead to many problems. Relations will be difficult.

Horse and Horse: With similar interests and outlooks, two Horses can get on well together.

Horse and Goat: Each will gain and learn much from the other. These two get on well.

Horse and Monkey: Despite their many fine qualities, these two tend to be distrustful of each other. Relations will be tricky.

Horse and Rooster: These two respect and admire each other but their forthright natures could lead to problems.

Horse and Dog: These two can build up an excellent rapport. They understand and trust each other well.

Horse and Pig: With their active and sociable natures, these two can become firm friends.

Goat and Goat: These two enjoy each other's company. They are well su ed.

Goat and Monkey: With care, these two can get on well and benefit from each other's strengths.

Goat and Rooster: Tricky. There is little rapport between them.

Goat and Dog: Their personalities are just so different. Relations will be difficult.

Goat and Pig: Their similar interests often bind them together. They get on well.

Monkey and Monkey: Sociable, enterprising and fun loving, these two get on marvellously.

Monkey and Rooster: Their personalities just clash. There will be little rapport.

Monkey and Dog: With some adjusting, these two can gain and learn much from each other.

Monkey and Pig: These two live and often enjoy life to the full. They get on well.

Rooster and Rooster: Candid, domineering, strong minded – relations will be far from easy.

Rooster and Dog: There are many differences between these two – and they know it. Relations will be difficult.

Rooster and Pig: These two can learn much from each other – but some adjusting is needed.

Dog and Dog: Loyal, trusting and affectionate. Relations between two Dogs will be good.

Dog and Pig: Loyal, caring and dependable, these two can strike up a good and meaningful rapport.

Pig and Pig: With similar interests, views and outlooks, two Pigs can get on marvellously.

The Chinese Years

Rat	31 January 1900	to	18 February 1901
Ox	19 February 1901	to	7 February 1902
Tiger	8 February 1902	to	28 January 1903
Rabbit	29 January 1903	to	15 February 1904
Dragon	16 February 1904	to	3 February 1905
Snake	4 February 1905	to	24 January 1906
Horse	25 January 1906	to	12 February 1907
Goat	13 February 1907	to	1 February 1908
Monkey	2 February 1908	to	21 January 1909
Rooster	22 January 1909	to	9 February 1910
Dog	10 February 1910	to	29 January 1911
Pig	30 January 1911	to	17 February 1912
Rat	18 February 1912	to	5 February 1913
Ox	6 February 1913	to	25 January 1914
Tiger	26 January 1914	to	13 February 1915
Rabbit	14 February 1915	to	2 February 1916
Dragon	3 February 1916	to	22 January 1917
Snake	23 January 1917	to	10 February 1918
Horse	11 February 1918	to	31 January 1919
Goat	1 February 1919	to	19 February 1920
Monkey	20 February 1920	to	7 February 1921
Rooster	8 February 1921	to	27 January 1922
Dog	28 January 1922	to	15 February 1923
Pig	16 February 1923	to	4 February 1924
Rat	5 February 1924	to	23 January 1925
Ox	24 January 1925	to	12 February 1926
Tiger	13 February 1926	to	1 February 1927
Rabbit	2 February 1927	to	22 January 1928
Dragon	23 January 1928	to	9 February 1929
Snake	10 February 1929	to	29 January 1930

Horse	30 January 1930	to	16 February 1931
Goat	17 February 1931	to	5 February 1932
Monkey	6 February 1932	to	25 January 1933
Rooster	26 January 1933	to	13 February 1934
Dog	14 February 1934	to	3 February 1935
Pig	4 February 1935	to	23 January 1936
Rat	24 January 1936	to	10 February 1937
Ox	11 February 1937	to	30 January 1938
Tiger	31 January 1938	to	18 February 1939
Rabbit	19 February 1939	to	7 February 1940
Dragon	8 February 1940	to	26 January 1941
Snake	27 January 1941	to	14 February 1942
Horse	15 February 1942	to	4 February 1943
Goat	5 February 1943	to	24 January 1944
Monkey	25 January 1944	to	12 February 1945
Rooster	13 February 1945	to	1 February 1946
Dog	2 February 1946	to	21 January 1947
Pig	22 January 1947	to	9 February 1948
Rat	10 February 1948	to	28 January 1949
Ox	29 January 1949	to	16 February 1950
Tiger	17 February 1950	to	5 February 1951
Rabbit	6 February 1951	to	26 January 1952
Dragon	27 January 1952	to	13 February 1953
Snake	14 February 1953	to	2 February 1954
Horse	3 February 1954	to	23 January 1955
Goat	24 January 1955	to	11 February 1956
Monkey	12 February 1956	to	30 January 1957
Rooster	31 January 1957	to	17 February 1958
Dog	18 February 1958	to	7 February 1959
Pig	8 February 1959	to	27 January 1960
Rat	28 January 1960	to	14 February 1961
Ox	15 February 1961	to	4 February 1962
Tiger	5 February 1962	to	24 January 1963
Rabbit	25 January 1963	to	12 February 1964
Dragon	13 February 1964	to	1 February 1965

Snake	2 February 1965	to	20 January 1966
Horse	21 January 1966	to	8 February 1967
Goat	9 February 1967	to	29 January 1968
Monkey	30 January 1968	to	16 February 1969
Rooster	17 February 1969	to	5 February 1970
Dog	6 February 1970	to	26 January 1971
Pig	27 January 1971	to	14 February 1972
Rat	15 February 19'2	to	2 February 1973
Ox	3 February 1973	to	22 January 1974
Tiger	23 January 1974	to	10 February 1975
Rabbit	11 February 1975	to	30 January 1976
Dragon	31 January 1976	to	17 February 1977
Snake	18 February 1977	to	6 February 1978
Horse	7 February 1978	to	27 January 1979
Goat	28 January 1979	to	15 February 1980
Monkey	16 February 1980	to	4 February 1981
Rooster	5 February 1981	to	24 January 1982
Dog	25 January 1982	to	12 February 1983
Pig	13 February 1983	to	1 February 1984
Rat	2 February 1984	to	19 February 1985
Ox	20 February 1985	to	8 February 1986
Tiger	9 February 1986	to	28 January 1987
Rabbit	29 January 1987	to	16 February 1988
Dragon	17 February 1988	to	5 February 1989
Snake	6 February 1989	to	26 January 1990
Horse	27 January 1990	to	14 February 1991
Goat	15 February 1991	to	3 February 1992
Monkey	4 February 1992	to	22 January 1993
Rooster	23 January 1993	to	9 February 1994
Dog	10 February 1994	to	30 January 1995
Pig	31 January 1995	to	18 February 1996
Rat	19 February 1996	to	6 February 1997
Ox	7 February 1997	to	27 January 1998
Tiger	28 January 1998	to	15 February 1999
Rabbit	16 February 1999	to	4 February 2000